THE
ESSENTIALS
OF
THEATER

THE
ESSENTIALS
OF
THEATER

A GUIDE TO ACTING, STAGECRAFT, TECHNICAL THEATER, AND MORE

LISA MULCAHY

ALLWORTH PRESS
NEW YORK

Allworth Press books may be purchased in bulk at special discounts for sales promotion, corporate gifts, fund-raising, or educational purposes. Special editions can also be created to specifications. For details, contact the Special Sales Department, Allworth Press, 307 West 36th Street, 11th Floor, New York, NY 10018 or info@skyhorsepublishing.com.

22 21 20 19 18   5 4 3 2 1

Published by Allworth Press, an imprint of Skyhorse Publishing, Inc. 307 West 36th Street, 11th Floor, New York, NY 10018. Allworth Press® is a registered trademark of Skyhorse Publishing, Inc.®, a Delaware corporation.

www.allworth.com

Cover design by Mary Ann Smith

Library of Congress Cataloging-in-Publication Data

Names: Mulcahy, Lisa, author.
Title: The essentials of theater : a guide to acting, stagecraft, technical theater, and more / Lisa Mulcahy.
Description: New York, New York : Allworth Press, [2018] | Includes index.
Identifiers: LCCN 2018019411 (print) | LCCN 2018029340 (ebook) | ISBN 9781621536475 (eBook) | ISBN 9781621536468 (hardcover : alk. paper)
Subjects: LCSH: Theater--Handbooks, manuals, etc. | Acting--Handbooks, manuals, etc. | Theater--Vocational guidance--Handbooks, manuals, etc.
Classification: LCC PN2037 (ebook) | LCC PN2037 .M85 2018 (print) | DDC 792--dc23
LC record available at https://lccn.loc.gov/2018019411

Print ISBN: 978-1-62153-646-8
eBook ISBN: 978-1-62153-647-5

Printed in the United States of America

For my parents, William and Joan Mulcahy

Contents

Acknowledgments

Great gratitude to the following terrific people for their support of this project:

Adrian Bridges; Ms. C.; Tad Crawford; James Foster Jr.; Mary Fitzgibbon; Robert Fitzgibbon; Meridith Friedman; Geoff Grammel of the Most Office in Fitchburg, Massachusetts; Chamois Holschuh; Debra Jeffries; Deborah Kelly; James Kelly; Ellen Mulcahy; Gloria Mulcahy; Sister Joan Mulcahy; John Rackliffe; Monique Rackliffe; Cherie B. Tay; Barry M. Willis; the posse; the Brandeis University theater arts department; and two very wonderful theater teachers, Ted Kazanoff and Edward Albee.

INTRODUCTION

What Is Theater Made Of?

What first attracted you to the idea of learning more about theater? For many students and aspiring professional thespians, the answer has to do with a memorable experience. For instance, so many performers have told me, during my long career as a theater journalist, that the impetus to jump in and learn more happened for them when they saw an exciting production as a young child and found themselves transfixed. Dazzled. Filled with awe and wonder and yearning to learn more about this new, emotional, sparkling onstage world before them.

Others, who are often humanities or English students, have expressed to me that academic interest drew them to want to learn about theater. After all, the art form is full of rich tradition, historical events and associations, deeply intelligent narrative, and highly technical performance mechanics that are endlessly fascinating to delve into. Plus, logically, today's dramaturgs and playwrights love to study the words and creative motivation of Shakespeare, of the Greeks, of the writers who crafted the template for plays that are still performed today. Modern directors and designers are also incredibly inspired by the staging of historical works and by the beauty and pageantry of costume and scenic progression over so many hundreds of years of theater history.

Then there are the passionate fans among us. Avid theatergoers who never miss a Broadway performance if they live in New York

City, or a regional or community theater production if they live in suburbia. Those folks who devour every biography they can find on theater actors, plays, and the craft of stage work. The more great theater you see, the more curious you tend to become about seeking out more of the communal experience it provides. You sit in a dark house experiencing a moving story and unfettered human emotion, and you share this as it's happening with an audience of peers. You're bonded to those peers, as well as to the performers you're viewing, in a very unique and powerful way.

Since you've decided to take a theater class or pick up this book, chances are very good you fit into one of the above three categories. Or maybe you don't; maybe you just need to get an arts requirement out of the way. That's cool, too. If you know practically nothing about theater at this moment, prepare to have your mind blown and your interest sparked. Why? Because in the process of working through this book, you'll grow to understand how theater positively impacts every one of us in society, through its fundamental function as an art form. You'll see for yourself how intriguing theater history can be, find yourself caught up in the personal success story of an accomplished theater artist, or surprise yourself with how much fun it is to take part in a theater exercise. Be prepared: theater hooks you fast.

This introduction is intended to inform you about the fundamental function of theater as an art form, and why it's important for us to understand its impact. Let's do this by answering some important questions.

Why Is Theater an Important Part of the Humanities Overall?

Theater has historically served as a societal "sounding board." Issues currently facing the world can be discussed in honest terms, with plenty of room for subjective interpretation and feedback, when you watch them play out in performance. Take, for example, the work of a genius playwright like Tony Kushner. Kushner's masterwork, *Angels in America*, which is referenced elsewhere in this book and which every theater student should be strongly encouraged to read, functions as a humanities lesson on numerous levels. First, it's an insightful exploration of how the AIDS crisis came to affect the world; next, it's a scathing political commentary regarding the pain that ignorance, selfishness, and false values have on the world we live in; and third, it's a deeply personal, sympathetic look at the victims of this disease and their loved ones. A controversial, beautiful, highly opinionated piece, it invokes emotion and thought in its readers and viewers and is the catalyst for important discussion. This play, and ambitious works like it, have the power to change minds and embolden people to take positive action throughout the world.

How Does Theater Work as an Art Form, and How Does It Inform Society?

Theater works as an art form because it's the epitome of complete freedom. A playmaker or performer can make any statement they like, perform a work in any style that feels truthful to them, and engage the audience as directly as they wish, and no choice is wrong. In the same vein, theater is a completely subjective art form to behold. You can watch it and love it; you can watch it and hate it. No matter—the point is, a point of view is unfolding before you, and you're reacting to it. This kind of give-and-take matters because it creates a dialogue (spoken or unspoken) between performer and viewer, and forces you, on one or more levels, to take a position.

Theater informs society because of this lack of mutual judgment. Whether you're infuriated by something you see onstage, whether your mind is changed by the content of a play, whether you learn something you never knew about yourself because you strongly identify with a character in a play—all of these emotions theater spawns create moments of personal growth. You change and learn about yourself through taking theater in, and expressing the new thought or reaction you have to someone else informs that person in a new way. You cause them to consider your opinion and form their *own* opinion of your point of view—one small societal change, one exchange at a time. The best way to foster this kind of positive discourse, naturally, happens when we take a friend to see a play and engage in a lively discussion about our thoughts on it after the performance is finished—an enlightening, expansive exercise if ever there was one.

How Can Theater Help Us Communicate?

Theater makes us brave. If we perform, we are baring our inner selves and our physical selves. We're vulnerable because we're expressing our emotions through a character wholeheartedly. If we direct or write a play, we're revealing our opinions on the stage or on the page in a way that can be extremely transparent and will often say a lot about our deepest beliefs and attitudes. If we design, we're sharing our artistic impulses and handiwork very overtly with the world—making a statement about how we see the world via the beautiful, or ugly, images and objects we create. All of these actions that thespians take in the name of their work are powerful communication tools, because courage speaks volumes and changes minds. Courage, when communicated, can inspire others to do something brave in turn, in their own lives. That's a meaningful gift thespians give that can play out in so many real-life scenarios beyond a theatrical experience.

What Can We Learn about Ourselves and Others from Participating in and/or Watching a Theatrical Piece?

We can appreciate that others live different lives than we do. We can understand larger issues in the world by seeing a play that explores these issues. We can open ourselves up to "trying" a new creative experience we don't think we're going to like (but end up loving the play we see in spite of ourselves). We can practice our critical thinking skills as we decide what we liked or didn't like about a play we've read or seen. We can see, while in the moment of experiencing the visual, aural, and sensory thrill of watching a good piece of drama, how wonderful it feels to be present and allow a memorable moment in our lives to influence us in a new way.

Why Does Studying Theater Provide Us with an Invaluable Understanding of Ourselves and the World We Live In?

Because of all of the above reasons, and one more: studying theater is a lot of fun! Reading about theater history is to enjoy learning about riveting times you never experienced art and culture in. Reading about the personal struggles and accomplishments of your favorite actress makes you more fully appreciate her amazing work when you watch her perform. And participating in theater to learn about it? It doesn't get any better than that.

USING THIS BOOK

Here's the purpose of each chapter presented for study in the book, with a view toward helping you understand the major concepts you'll learn. We're about to cover the following:

- Theater history
- Theater terminology
- Text analysis
- Acting
- Directing
- Playwrighting
- Design
- Technical theater work
- Ways to apply theater study to a variety of careers, both show business–related and in other industries

We'll also outline a complete chapter for a four-week production you and your classmates and teacher can take on—a very valuable and enriching opportunity.

Many chapters feature "Selected Readings"—lesson-oriented articles that expand on the major topic we've covered in entertaining and informative detail. You can use these readings as supplementary food for thought, as inspiration for your own paper or project on a particularly interesting theater maker or piece of well-known theatrical material—really, any way you see fit. The more you know, the more color will be added to your understanding of theatrical process and creativity.

You'll also note that some chapters contain worksheets. Essentially, these worksheets are writing exercises intended to help further foster your understanding of theatrical detail. For example, in chapter 1, the worksheet assignment given has to do with researching and writing about a theater festival known for its rich street theater element, a direct offshoot of some basic reading you'll do in the chapter about street theater as a whole topic.

If you choose to tackle a worksheet, or are assigned to do so, there's no specific intention as to how long your written exercise/essay should be in regard to covering the topic—I would say 750–1,000 words will be a good recommendation, however, in terms of enhancing your comprehension of the subject you're writing about.

Finally, at the end of many chapters, you'll find a "Chapter Checklist"—suggestions for interactive ways you can practice the points of a theater study topic you've just learned about in that section.

There's lots to do—so let's begin. I'm delighted to embark on this journey with you!

—Lisa Mulcahy
2018

PART ONE

Core Coverage

1

A Little History, Please

As a rule, all modern theater is steeped in the past—it's an art form rich in tradition. And that's a good thing. Yet you're probably thinking, isn't the theater we see today so fascinating because it's always changing and evolving? Isn't the point to keep things as fresh as possible, so theatrical creativity can really flourish?

Absolutely—and theater is such a free, cutting-edge mode of expression, we are always seeing new concepts and performance innovation, everywhere from the most bare-bones student production to a lushly experimental show in New York. The history of theatrical writing, movement, and theory, however, remain a huge influence on the work thespians do today. So many elements of theatrical execution—such as the way actors use their bodies or the rhythms in which playwrights craft their texts—have their roots in historic theatrical genres.

In this chapter, let's take a focused look at how theater was first physically created and performed. We'll cover the specifics of four historical genres—Greek theater, Kabuki theater, Elizabethan Renaissance theater, and commedia dell'arte—and pay tribute to each genre's innovators throughout theatrical history. Each of these genres is still performed throughout the world today, and so many thespians incorporate elements of each form innately today. Take, for example, any contemporary comedy or tragedy—arguably, its roots can be clearly seen in the major themes pioneered by the Greeks, who were the chief architects of the examination of highly emotional subject matter in a dramatic context. As you read about each historic genre, you'll be struck by the similarities you notice in terms of ideas, techniques, and styles practiced theatrically in the past and in the theater we see and do today. Everything comes full circle, and always will.

GET ME TO THE GREEKS: THE PROGRESSION OF GREEK THEATER

Dramatic productions in ancient Greece started to crop up around 700 BC in Athens. Festivals such as the Dionysia became the introductory platform for the basic premise of Greek performance, which encompassed three major genres: tragedy, comedy, and satire (known as *satyr*—and defined as spoofing dramatic subject matter). The public cottoned to Greek theater pretty much right away, due to the fact that one-on-one and group storytelling was a very common component of the culture at this time.

Thespis, an actor specializing in dramatic tales of woe, became Greek theater's first true superstar—he was known as the "Father of Tragedy," in that he guided the productions of many a tear-jerking performance. Another Greek thespian, Solon, specialized in creating poems and spoken-word performances. Greek theater's most respected early producer was Phrynichus, who worked to help stage tragedies such as *Capture of Miletus*. Interest in Greek theater began to truly accelerate when three highly regarded thinkers and playwrights, Aristotle, Aeschylus, and Sophocles, began writing plays in a competition to try to outdo each other with their best individual work. Another respected writer, Menander, was instrumental in launching the New

Comedy period that proved to be an enduring success, with audiences enjoying a number of humorous new works.

Actors had plentiful opportunities to work in Greek theater—each play usually had twelve to fifteen chorus roles, in addition to lead parts. Only two to three actors were ever onstage at a single moment, however, so often, one actor would take on multiple roles—even in a single scene—which required significant concentration and talent. No female thespians were allowed to perform in Greek plays at the time, though—men played all the female characters. Any time a character in a play died, they did so offstage, because Greek playwrights believed audiences were too fragile to actually witness any character's demise directly. Musicians could also find opportunity to work on these productions, as most plays were elaborately scored. And audiences got plenty of dramatic and comedic excitement for their attendance—performances traditionally lasted for entire days, from morning to night! Another interesting element of Greek performance: beautifully expressive masks, depicting comedy and tragedy faces, were frequently used as "costuming" in plays. Masks were considered a crucial tool in helping the audience understand the subtext of the material they were watching, and often donned to define clarity in a scene, or comment visually on the action. In the evening, at the end of each marathon show, any masks worn by the actors in a play were formally dedicated at an altar of the Greek god Dionysus. Luxurious headgear was also a staple of Greek costuming; masks were often built with lush wigs streaming human or animal hair or with ornate helmets attached. A final common accessory: extremely tall boots, called *cothurni*, created the illusion of height for many actors, and allowed audiences at any area of the performance space to better see the performers.

Speaking of the Greek performance space: it was always constructed as an amphitheater. Essentially, a Greek amphitheater stage was a round space measuring roughly seventy-eight feet in diameter. Amphitheaters were traditionally built at the base of a hill, with a rounded seating setup that ascended up that hill; many audience members, as a result, were looking down at the performance from wood or stone seating.

Onstage, each piece of a Greek amphitheater set was designed with the intention to maximize sightlines for the audience. The *logeion*, a tall platform, was a key component of every play's set design—it was used by each actor as a dominant spot from which to deliver a speech. The entrances actors used, called the *paradoi* or *eisodoi*, were multiple stories high; matching their height were *thyromata*, or painted images that illustrated the themes of each play. The *paraskenia*, a stone wall segment of the stage, was a major visual element, as was a rudimentary crane, which was used to fly in pieces of scenery. Platforms on wheels were another, easier way to move painted scenery and props on- and offstage. Everything was *big*, and it needed to be, in order to accommodate incredible crowd sizes—up to fourteen thousand people would rush to each performance!

ELEGANT PHYSICALITY: KABUKI THEATER

In 1603, an astoundingly beautiful new art form began in Japan. Kabuki, best described as dramatic performance colored extensively by dance movements, came to be. *Kabuki* translates to English as "to lean" (which is evident in many of its signature physical movements) and "to be out of the ordinary"—which this special theatrical genre certainly is.

Kabuki's godmother, arguably, was Izumo no Okuni, who started staging original dances in dry riverbeds throughout the city of Kyoto. Kabuki provided a great opportunity for women to pursue creative expression, as it was only performed by female performers initially. Once word got out about the lovely original work being done by Okuni and other Kabuki artists, the form moved to other Japanese cities, specifically Edo, and became so popular that performances were given for the Imperial Court. Kabuki ensembles started to come together all across the country.

One of the most recognizable signatures of Kabuki was thick whiteface makeup, made of rice powder, which was applied in a linear, very detailed manner called *kumadori* and altered to reflect the character being interpreted. Japanese current events became staple subject matter of Kabuki—material for performances included fashion and historical/social/political events. Shows could last from early morning to nighttime and contained five distinct acts: *jo* (act one, which slowly set up the performance's premise), *ha* (acts two, three and four, a faster progression of the story line), and *kyu* (act five, a brief ending to the performance). Set pieces that were most relevant to Kabuki productions included revolving stages, flies, trapdoors, and mini "wagons," small wheeled stages that could quickly set up or remove pieces of scenery.

Actors would strike distinct poses in performance: the *mie* was a key pose that visually determined the essence of a character for the audience. By the mid-1600s, men had begun forming all-male Kabuki troupes, and drama began to take hold as Kabuki's major hallmark, phasing out the dance aspect. Kabuki's most popular and artistically significant period was 1673–1841; works such as *The Love Suicides at Amijima* by Chikamatsu Monzaemon sparked controversy as well as creative growth. Kawatake Mokuami started writing Kabuki plays about the life of the everyday man, adding music to his material's presentations as well.

Kabuki flourished for centuries; however, after World War II, it was briefly outlawed in Japan, as some people objected to its traditional themes from the country's past. Director Tetsuji Takechi was undaunted, however, and began restaging classic Kabuki plays. Today, all eras of Kabuki are revered in Japan and by thespians all over the world—the performance style can be found in theaters in Tokyo, Kyoto, and Osaka, as well as enjoyed by audiences worldwide via well-respected touring companies.

POWER TO THE PEOPLE: ENGLISH RENAISSANCE THEATER

English Renaissance theater, (also known as Elizabethan theater) was vastly popular between the years of 1562 and 1642, starting in the early years of and lasting beyond Queen Elizabeth I's reign. It was considered a democratic mode for presenting new works, in that it was "public." This meant English Renaissance productions could be enjoyed by all classes of English society—at a performance, you could often spot a member of the royal family in the audience, surrounded by commoners.

Big public theater spaces very quickly started cropping up outside of London (where private theater had always been the rule, and exclusively for the upper echelon of society), then throughout the country, due to the great popularity of plays in England during the Renaissance era. These facilities swiftly became big moneymakers; houses with especially good revenue included the Theatre in Shoreditch, the Curtain Theatre, the Swan, the Fortune, the Globe, and the Red Bull. Most of these houses boasted an open-roof space, with a performance area at its center containing platforming and a balcony, although several additional English Renaissance houses, including Salisbury Court Theatre and the Cockpit, were opened with traditional roofing. Such theaters operated on the repertory system—no single play ran on two consecutive days. Production values were bare bones: there were no sets to speak of, and lighting was achieved via candlelight or simply outdoor light seeping into the performance space.

The primary theme of English Renaissance plays tended to be variations on high-stakes tragedy, often with a revenge-driven plot twist. Playwrights like William Shakespeare, Thomas Dekker, Thomas Kyd, and Ben Jonson saw their careers flourish by churning out these extremely dramatic works. A famous play that falls very much in line with this edict is *Doctor Faustus* by Christopher Marlowe, in which a man sells his soul to the devil; other wildly entertaining revenge tragedies included *The Spanish Tragedy* and *The Duchess of Malfi*. Interest in these and other works spread back to London, and finally, by 1580, the rules against public theater were lifted. English Renaissance theater came to the capital city; to honor the aristocracy who now attended performances, purple, the color of royalty, was woven into the actors' costumes. All was well . . .

. . . until 1642. At that time, the powerful Puritans declared theater to be a sinful creative form and outlawed it. Theater spaces closed, and actors were put out of work, sadly. But the plays? They live on today, as some of the most creative, beguiling, and insightful written words ever committed to the page.

GOING FOR THE LAUGH: COMMEDIA DELL'ARTE

In Italian, the phrase *commedia dell'arte* means "comedy of the profession"—and this influential theatrical form, which dates all the way back to the Roman Republic period, certainly coaxed laughs out of its viewers. Both scripted and improvised, commedia dell'arte integrated stereotypical characters into broad sketches full of pantomime and big human themes.

Although not a lot of historical data is available, the first commedia dell'arte play is believed to have been produced in 1551, in a street performance (although later on, indoor performances were held throughout Italy). Commedia dell'arte focused on emotionally charged, wildly exaggerated comic situations dealing with subjects like love and greed. A harlequin character, Arlecchino, was often central to the themes of many story lines. Other stock characters included Il Dottore (the Doctor), *vecchi* (two elderly men) and *innamorata* (two pairings of lovers). Acting troupes were formed to interpret these plays, including the Gelosi, Confidenti, and Accessi theater companies. Women were fully involved in performing roles in commedia dell'arte, and story lines of each play were often updated to reflect local events when a troupe played in a certain city or town. Commedia dell'arte technique was said to be a big inspiration for the creation of Punch and Judy's puppet plays, and eventually, in addition to the standardized slapstick and jokes in each play, some elements of tragedy were included in the material, as the art form grew artistically.

Today, many advanced acting classes in master of fine arts programs immerse students in the commedia dell'arte technique, as it's so different from more subtle forms of Method acting that are so standardized today. Commedia dell'arte is a really effective way for an actor to learn a sense of controlled physical and emotional chaos, if you will—a freedom that can be a powerful skill in building any character.

——————SELECTED READINGS——————

Here's more information on intriguing theatrical subtypes that are inform and inspire today's theatrical artists.

No Words Speak Volumes

The concept of mime is one of the theater's most expressive and enduring art forms. You probably know that mime means a performer is mute and uses his or her body to communicate the ideas of a particular scene or situation.

Here's where mime originated from, and how it's done when it's done right.

The method we've come to know as mime actually started in ancient Greece, where actors used their bodies to silently act out a story in some public performances. This raw style of performance really flourished, however, in nineteenth-century Paris. Mimes (who, by the way, were originally called "mummers") began to hone their technique by drawing upon fluid dance movements as inspiration. Certain physical gestures—leaning, using the hands in very detailed and precise ways to indicate a particular action, and adopting exaggerated facial expressions to convey emotions—became the gold standard. Mimes also universally adopted the use of the whiteface makeup palette in Paris at this time: a stark, snowy foundation enhanced by black-rimmed eyes and colorfully painted lips.

Mimes who were considered masters in terms of teaching others, and inventing new ways to interpret scenarios through mime, included Jean Soubeyran, Brigitte Soubeyran, Jean-Gaspard Deburau, Jacques Lecoq, and Etienne Decroux. Marcel Marceau brought mime into popular culture, often appearing onstage and on television in Europe and the United States in the 1960s and 1970s as his charming character Bip. Interestingly, Charlie Chaplin was considered the first mime in the world of cinema, having studied and adapted many elements of mime within his silent film work. Harpo Marx was also considered to be drawing significantly from the art form in honing his nonspeaking roles in the Marx Brothers films; Buster Keaton and Dario Fo also incorporated aspects of mime into their film and stage work. And that continues today. Popular actress Isla Fisher (from the films *The Wedding Crashers* and *Keeping Up with the Joneses*), developed her gift for physical comedy through mime study—proof that the practical foundations of silent acting skill endure very effectively.

Taking It to the Streets: The Allure of Street Theater

Got a great idea for a show? Head down the block to that empty parking lot and start acting your little heart out.

Seriously, it's a valid option—street theater is considered an esteemed dramatic genre all over the world, is dirt cheap in terms of overhead, and allows an actor to stretch his or her imagination infinitely—the location you choose is the measure of how resourceful you can be as a playmaker.

The history of street theater speaks to the power of rebellion. A most fascinating example of this has to do with the rich tapestry of street theater as it evolved in India. Sanskrit theater, performed in public places, began in the country in the second century BC, emphasizing early social concerns. As the years passed, Indian street theater grew more creatively complex, using puppetry as a key component. Political street theater started to make a populist impact in 1949, with the vastly popular play *Chargesheet*, performed in Calcutta. Workers embraced the art form, as it often spoke to their grassroots concerns, including uprisings and protest. Indeed, well-known street theater troupes such as Janam and Samudaya were established in the 1970s, churning out literally thousands of politically themed productions. Street theater has also enjoyed immense popularity worldwide, specifically in Eastern Europe, the UK, and Canada.

To give a great street theater performance, you can work on a street corner, on a subway platform, in a public park—anywhere you can draw a crowd, really. Sets obviously must be kept to a minimum, so most crafty street performers choose to incorporate the environment they're in throughout the artistic statement they're making. Busking—or "passing the hat"—is a very important and lucrative endeavor for many street performers. It refers to collecting money from audience members and passersby. Many professional street performers actually earn a living from busking, as well as by affiliation with one of hundreds of theater festivals that support street theater as an importance aspect of their performance schedules. The annual Edinburgh Festival Fringe in Scotland enthusiastically encourages its participants to do street theater if the spirit moves, for example. "Guerrilla" street theater troupes, such as the Bread and Puppet Theatre and the San Francisco Mime troupe, both in the US, are known for sophisticated and intelligent street theater performances that, as befitting the form's history, speak to a community's political viewpoints. And street theater is a great way to learn how to establish a big, bold presence as a performer—both David Bowie and Robin Williams got their starts this way.

————WORKSHEET ASSIGNMENT————

Read up on and write a summary of the Edinburgh Festival Fringe in Edinburgh, Scotland. This freewheeling fest boasts street theater at its most boisterous, and is heaven-sent for scores of buskers, who collect money from festivalgoers and locals like there's no tomorrow.

———————— CHAPTER 1 CHECKLIST————————

Get more out of what you've learned in this chapter by:

☐ Reading the Greek tragedy *Antigone* by Sophocles. It's a juicy, ancient-era soap opera complete with family drama, strife, agony, passion—an example of the emotional elements this genre so skillfully employs to move the reader and/or viewer.

☐ Watching *Henry V*, directed by Kenneth Branagh. This 1989 film adaptation of Shakespeare's classic work is fiery, touching, and unforgettable. Branagh is considered one of the Bard's most illustrious interpreters today, and his affinity for the material is wildly evident in both his guidance of the film and his Oscar-nominated performance in the title role. Strong acting from Emma Thompson as well.

☐ Trying Mirror Mime. This acting exercise will help you recognize the importance of detailed movement, as is used in mime, as you both practice it and observe it at the same time. Grab a classmate, then face each other in a standing position. Choose who will lead this exercise; that person begins a movement—something as simple as raising a hand over his or her head. The other person mirrors this movement as specifically as possible. Then the second person initiates a movement, and the first person mirrors their movement. Continue the back-and-forth, utilizing and moving your arms, legs, eyebrows—anything you want to try. As you get into a groove, your movements will start to flow in unison—very cool indeed!

2

How to Speak Theater

When you're first immersed in the environment of putting on a play, one thing might seem especially complicated, and more than a little confusing: the language of theater. Everywhere you listen, people are talking about "going up" and "striking" and being "off-book" so casually, it might seem like you're looking in on a really cool club of which you're too illiterate to be a member. This is so not true! Learning the lingo of thespians is actually a lot easier than it seems.

Sure, it's true that theater is one of those working areas where very specific theatrical terms, jargon, and vocabulary are essential in order to participate effectively when working on a production. The good news, though, is that as you learn these theatrical words and phrases, you also rather effortlessly learn the basic definitions of stage directions, stage locations/areas, and production functions. With this knowledge, you can competently act or work on a crew and even read and understand the text of a play with greater clarity.

Theatrical terminology is also important to know because it's a crucial link in the chain of camaraderie that makes up every show, everywhere. Theater slang is truly a "secret handshake": when you use it properly, it forms a quick bond with your coworkers on a play and earns you their respect as an informed equal.

So how do you start talking the talk? Familiarize yourself with the following list of terms and their definitions.

THEATER VOCABULARY LIST

(Make it your business to know them all.)

A Capella—Singing without any instrumental backing.

Ad Lib—An improvised bit of dialogue in an audition, rehearsal, or performance.

Aside—"Commenting" through dialogue or action directly to the audience during a scene.

Beat—A pause in a scene that enhances its impact or message.

Belt—Singing strongly from the diaphragm. Also called "using your chest voice."

Black Box—A small (ninety-nine seats or under) theater space, usually rimmed with black curtains.

Blackout—All lights go out in the theater and onstage—usually happens at the end of a scene or act.

Blacks—Black curtains hung on the sides or back of a stage.

Blocking—The process of planning out how actors will move around the stage throughout the course of the play.

Book—The script of a play.

Business—Incidental activity onstage during a scene. Example: a waiter clearing a table stage left (SL) as a dialogue scene plays center stage is doing business.

Call Time—The hour at which cast members must report to the theater before a performance.

Callboard—A wall area for posting notices backstage at the theater.

Calling the Show—The process of the stage manager reading all lighting, sound, and set promptings over headphones during a performance to the technical crew members.

Catwalk—A bridge-like steel suspension high over the stage and house that lighting equipment is often hung from.

Center Stage—The middle of the stage. Arguably the most dominant stage location.

Cheat—Turning an actor, or set piece, at a slight angle so there's better visibility for the audience.

Chorus—A group of actors in a musical who sing in unison and back up the lead performers.

Cold Reading—Auditioning without having ever seen the text you're reading before.

Contact Sheet—A list distributed to cast and crew of all personnel's phone and email addresses.

Costume Fitting—Trying a nearly completed costume on an actor so adjustments can be made.

Costume Parade—Actors wear their finished costumes under the stage lights to determine if any last-minute wardrobe tweaks are needed.

Count—A timing call stage managers use to ensure cues are executed at the right places in a show.

Crashbox—A box packed with objects like bells or silverware that will make a big amount of noise offstage when dropped or shaken, as a sound effect for a show.

Crossover—When actors walk across the stage, or crew members move scenery in a coordinated manner during a performance.

Cues—Lighting, sound, and technical actions that the stage manager gives during a performance.

Downstage—The front of the stage, closest to the audience.

Dry Tech—A technical rehearsal that doesn't include actors.

Ensemble—A group of actors in a drama, usually with nonspeaking roles.

Entrance—Walking onstage.

Exit—Walking offstage.

Flat—A freestanding wooden set piece that can be painted as part of the set and can be positioned anywhere onstage.

Flies—Any rigged piece of scenery that is dropped in by cables onstage.

Fourth Wall—The invisible separation that keeps an actor's focus within a scene, not looking or playing directly to the audience.

Go: The command the stage member gives to the crew so a cue is executed.

House—Where the audience sits.

Load-In—Putting up a set before a production opens.

Masking—Covering specific areas of the stage with blacks as part of a show's design or set configuration.

Note—A comment or criticism given to an actor or crew members regarding their work.

Photo Call—Still pictures are taken of specific scene moments, with actors in full costume and on the completed set.

Pit—Where the orchestra plays.

Places—The spots onstage or in the wings where actors wait at the start of the performance.

Prep Crew—A group of costume or set workers who prepare the elements of a production during the rehearsal period.

Projection—A vocal/breathing technique that actors use to speak loudly so everyone in the audience can hear and understand them.

Promptbook—The stage manager's annotated book, complete with all essential info about a show.

Quick Change—The speedy process of an actor changing costumes offstage—often with only seconds to do it in.

Read-Through—A cast meeting, usually around a table, at which the script of a play is read aloud for the first time.

Run Crew—A group of costume or set workers who execute the elements of a production during the performance period.

Run-Through—A scene-by-scene rough performance of a play toward the end of the rehearsal period.

Sides—Portion or portions of a script actors use to audition with.

SL—Stage left. "Left" refers to the actor's left side.

Spike the Stage—Using glow tape to mark the position of set pieces on the floor of a stage for rehearsal and performance.

SR—Stage right. "Right" refers to the actor's right side.

Stakes—The motivating factors in a scene that actors use in order to establish logical action for their characters.

Strike—Taking down a set once a production closes.

Understudy—An actor who learns a principal role in case the actor who has that role officially can't perform.

Upstage—The back of the stage, farthest from the audience.

Walk-On—An extra making a brief appearance in a play.

Warm-Up—The process of actors exercising their voices and bodies before a rehearsal or performance.

Wet Tech—A technical rehearsal that does include actors.

Wings—The offstage side areas where actors wait for entrances, crew members work, and set pieces stand at the ready.

Work Lights/Blues—Small, highly illuminating lights that the stage manager and crew use to work in dark spots offstage during a performance.

ESSENTIAL SLANG

(Drop these terms to sound like a real pro.)

ASM—Assistant stage manager.

Call for a Line—Saying "line" during a rehearsal means you've forgotten your next piece of dialogue; the stage manager (SM) or ASM will prompt you.

Curtain Call—The cast's big bow for applause at the end of every performance. They deserve it!

Dance Captain—A cast member of a musical who helps the choreographer run dance routines with the rest of the performers.

Dark—The day of the week a show isn't performed, so cast and crew have a break.

Dress—The final rehearsal, with all technical elements included, before a show opens.

Equity—Short for Actors Equity Association, the stage performers' union.

Go Up—The date the show opens.

ME—Master electrician: supervisor of the lighting crew.

Off-Book—rehearsing without your script, because you know your lines by heart.

On-Book—Reading directly from your script during rehearsal, because you haven't memorized your lines yet.

Put Up—To stage the show.

SFX—Special effects.

SM—Stage manager.

Walk-through—Quickly performing the dialogue and blocking of a show in rehearsal so everyone grasps these basic elements.

SELECTED READINGS

Talking the Talk (and Doing the Job): An Interview with Stage Manager Cherie B. Tay

Someone who is very fluent in the language of theater would be an accomplished professional stage manager. Let's meet Cherie B. Tay, who has distinguished herself as an SM in regional theater, on touring shows, and on Broadway. Cherie is a graduate of the prestigious University of the Arts in London; she's worked at numerous Philadelphia theater companies and was a stage manager on the second national tour of *In the Heights*. She also worked as a stage manager for the North American and Tokyo tours of *War Horse*, and on the Great White Way's production of *Amélie*. Here, Cherie tells us about how she's come to ply her trade. Notice how she uses a number of the phrases we've discussed as she expertly describes the technical aspect of her job.

Q: Could you talk a bit about how you decided to become a stage manager? What experiences or influences started you on this journey?

A: It was not a straight path, for sure. My parents took me to touring Broadway shows when I was younger, which is where my love of theater started. In ninth grade, I was asked to pull curtains for the fall play and I ended up stage-managing every year in high school. I went to college for stage management, did an apprenticeship, then started working professionally in Philadelphia. While in college, I loaded in and shadowed touring Broadway shows, which is where I met an SM who later pulled me onto the *War Horse* tour. After SMing the *In the Heights* tour, the orchestrator pulled me to be his music assistant on *Bring It On* for Broadway. I then went on to music assist more shows, which is where I met my current PM, Jim Harker. We've now worked together for three years. He has been a huge inspiration to me.

Q: How do you, as an SM, approach the task of managing different personalities and perspectives within the company of a show—i.e., helping different folks like designers, the director, and actors work together most fruitfully?

A: It's a lot of listening and paying attention. You'll have to figure out how each person communicates and translate it so that everyone is on the same page.

Q: Any tips for new stage managers regarding the daunting task of calling a show? Any technical tricks you might want to share would be great.

A: It helps to put an asterisk or some sort of mark in the script to notate when to start saying the cue. Call your warnings in the sequence order. "GO" is always last. Don't say "GO, lights, four." It's "Lights four, GO." Try to keep the same pace when saying cues. Try not to "Lights, four . . . nnnnnGO," then "Lights-five-GO!!" Keep your fingers on the cue switches if you have a cue coming up, so you don't have to try and find the switches right before they should trigger.

Q: What has been your most rewarding experience thus far as a stage manager?

A: Being in the room and helping the show develop and come together. Solving complicated sequences and having them run smoothly. Knowing that people depend on you and trust you. Helping and teaching young stage managers.

Breaking a Leg: Saying Good Luck Is Bad Luck

Whatever you do . . . no matter how much you want to . . . *never* wish an actor friend of yours good luck on opening night. Or any time, for that matter, while they're working on a play in any stage of development. Nope. Don't even think about it.

Why? Because in the theater, the term *good luck* has a nasty reputation for bringing the exact opposite kind of fortune to any thespian it's said to and could doom his or her performance or production.

Instead, superstition dictates you should say, "Break a leg." Sounds dangerous, but it's actually considered a precursor of great fortune for an actor and his or her show as a whole. Why? Let's take a fun, historical look at four reasons why "breaking a leg" came to be universally accepted as the safe way to wish an actor well:

- **It means the actor's really going to kill it.** Back in the eighteenth century, actor David Garrick literally broke his leg during an intense stage performance in *Richard III*—he was so involved in the moment and in his work, lore has it he didn't even feel the pain. So saying "break a leg" can be the same as telling an actor, "You're going to do a fantastic job!"
- **It can wish the actor a bigger payday.** Back in the age of vaudeville performances, any time your leg could be seen breaking past a curtain and appearing onstage, you got extra cash. "Breaking a leg" therefore expresses a wish for an actor's prosperity.
- **It indicates you hope the whole show will go well.** When actors bow at the end of a show to the audience's applause, they "break" their normal standing position and often bend their legs slightly. Over the years, the term "break a leg" became related to bowing after an overall successful performance for that reason.

- **It uses reverse psychology in a good way.** Some actors simply believe if you wish someone bad luck, the opposite result will happen. True? Who knows? Better not tempt fate (or lose a friend)—just say the words, and hope for the best.

Never Say "Macbeth," or Something Else You Should Avoid Saying in a Theater

Speaking of more words you never knew you shouldn't utter—don't say the name of Shakespeare's famous play in any theatrical space, ever. The reason: the play itself is supposed to be cursed—the precise details as to how that happened are unclear. Still, if you're in the play and speak the title outside an actual performance, you are guaranteeing yourself misery and failure onstage, according to widely observed theatrical tradition.

It's OK to call the show "the Scottish Play" while you're at the theater, though. And you can say "Macbeth" away from your venue. But you should never run lines before a performance to further avoid bad luck, especially any dialogue that the witches in the text recite.

What if you accidentally blurt the Title That Shall Be Unnamed, despite all of your best efforts? Walk out of the theater, spin in a circle three times, spit, say your favorite swearword, and then knock exactly three times on the stage door to be let back inside the building. Voilà—disaster averted!

WORKSHEET ASSIGNMENT

Write out all of the terminology listed in this chapter. Yep, hand-write it. There's no better way to get vocabulary into your bones than by copying it down the old-fashioned way. Now stash the entire list somewhere on your person and memorize the list over the course of two to three days. One of your classmates or several classmates should do the same. Got everything stored in your brain? Good. Grab a few minutes with your friends, and quiz yourselves to make sure everyone has the terminology officially cemented.

———— CHAPTER 2 CHECKLIST ————

Get more out of what you've learned in this chapter by:

☐ Watching *Birdman, or the Unexpected Virtue of Ignorance*, directed by Alejandro G. Iñárritu. The winner of the 2014 Best Picture Oscar, this film gives a real sense of the atmosphere of working in the theater and demonstrates how a director, actors, and crew members communicate with each other. Great performances by Michael Keaton, Edward Norton, Emma Stone, Naomi Watts, Andrea Riseborough, Zach Galifianakis, and Amy Ryan.

☐ Shadowing the SM of a production at your school. Ask if you may observe him/her work through a rehearsal—this is an excellent way to hear theater talk in real time and offers you the chance to watch the SM carry out the technical tasks essential to a play.

☐ Memorize the terminology we've covered. Read the listings over a number of times to become comfortable with each term and its meaning. Then commit the listings to memory. Next, grab a friend from class and quiz each other till you both know each term cold. Finally, practice is the easiest way to retain what you've learned. Use these terms often, in class or at play rehearsal or simply in conversation with your fellow students so theater speak becomes second nature to everyone.

3

Text, and How to Really Get It

When it comes to understanding a script, a lot of the work is actually pretty self-explanatory. Reading a play for plot, content, and character information should always feel like reading a really good novel, if the playwright has done his or her job well. In your mind's eye, as you read, you should immediately be able to see the world the playwright is describing: it should be easy to visualize the way a character moves, speaks, and sounds, too. Play text has a lot to do with a story, of course, but it's also essential that a playwright convey a strong sense of atmosphere, of place and time, and a sense of the human qualities that help us understand, root for, or root against each character that's depicted within that story.

So, quite obviously, text analysis and comprehension of a script is pretty darn important, so you, as a reader, can fully absorb the themes and technical points of any given play. Let's break down the elements of a play's text, part by part, so you will be well prepared the next time you look at a play on the page.

FULL-LENGTH PLAY STRUCTURE

A full-length play (either a dramatic or comic play or a musical) is most often made up of two acts of relatively similar length. Each act consists of a number of scenes (usually around five to seven). Each page of the play equals roughly one minute of stage time. The setting of a play is clearly established at the top of each act and is adjusted clearly within the play's text if that setting changes. The play's plot is its logical story, from beginning to end.

A full-length play consists of a title page, which lists the play's title and author as follows:

The High School Friendship
by Grade A. Playwright

Next, there'll be a cast of characters page. This is the playwright's chance to set up some basic information (for readers of the play, as well as the actors and director who will bring the play to life) about the identifying traits, physical appearance, and personal circumstances of each character.

Here's an example of how that page might look, with two sample characters in a fictitious high school play:

Cast of Characters

Kirsten—Fourteen years old. Shy schoolgirl trying to make friends in a new, intimidating environment.
Ashley—Fifteen years old. Confident, comfortable student who seeks to become Kirsten's friend.

From these thumbnail descriptions, you can get a sense of the stakes both the characters of Kirsten and Ashley experience within the play, plus what they want. How they will go after what they each want will comprise their individual arcs—an arc is the road map each character follows to meet her goals and develop as a person, throughout the play's progression.

THEMES AND SCENES WORKING TOGETHER

The play should have an overall theme that's "bigger" than the plot itself—a statement that the playwright wants to make about an issue. The action of the play illustrates the theme in action.

Here's how it works. Let's say we decide that the theme of our fictitious high school play is courage in the face of rejection. Each scene of the play should reflect this theme as it moves the overall story forward sensibly, and without a lot of complicated distractions like dialogue that goes off on a tangent or too many unneeded characters spinning around the edges of each scene. For our sample play here, the plot is whether Kirsten will be able to overcome her shyness to make friends and thrive at her new school—will she accept Ashley's friendship? OK, so that's the basic idea we follow throughout each scene, until we reach the play's apex, and discover whether Kirsten did or did not achieve her goal of success. Of course, other characters can come along and act as obstacles to her goal—such as a bully who tries to get other popular students to reject her. Hey, that's an interesting plot point, because it can be a strong motivator for Ashley's character. Will Ashley have the courage to stand up to this bully and support Kirsten, even if it means her own status within the popular crowd will be threatened?

FORMAT

So what does the play look like laid out on the page? Here's an example of basic play format.

Title: Act One, Scene One

Setting: A busy school cafeteria. Students are talking loudly, laughing boisterously, and eating in groups at tables.

ENTER KIRSTEN, a freshman who's just transferred here from across the country. She looks around nervously, takes a seat by herself, and quickly opens the brown bag she's carrying. Kirsten removes a sandwich from her bag, unwraps it, and starts eating quickly, with birdlike bites, looking down at the table in front of her.

ENTER ASHLEY, a popular sophomore. She strolls from stage right past Kirsten's table, then pauses and turns back to address the solitary student.

ASHLEY (in a friendly tone): Hi, I'm Ashley! I love your hair! I wish mine was long like yours.

KIRSTEN (almost inaudible): Thanks. I should have washed it today.

ASHLEY: What? I think it looks great! So, you know what, I think we have French class together. What's your name?

KIRSTEN (in a whisper): Kirsten.

ASHLEY: Oh, hi, Kirsten. Listen, you don't have to sit here by yourself. Some of the other girls and I are going to eat outside on the lawn, because it's such a beautiful day. Want to come?

KIRSTEN (smiling with relief, her voice stronger now): OK. Thanks.

Note the importance of natural-sounding dialogue within a scene. The way each character in a play speaks should be reflective of the specifics of their character. As you can see from the example above, Kirsten's dialogue reflects her insecurity and lack of self-confidence, while Ashley's dialogue is positive and more effervescent. You'll find more detailed info, and a great dialogue exercise, coming up in chapter 6.

BUILDING TOWARD THE CLIMAX

As the play progresses, the obstacles your characters face should be very specific, and visually clear to the audience. For example, the bully that is threatening Kirsten could push her, steal the homework out of her bag—do something very definitive so that when Ashley and Kirsten face off against this bully, there is a genuine dramatic reason to do so. The more specific your obstacles are from a physical standpoint as well, the more the overall dramatic tension will ramp up. This will make the ending of the play an emotional and visceral success.

HOW DO YOU KNOW IF A PLAY READS THE "RIGHT" WAY?

The truth is, there is no "right" way for a play to read. Within the basic structure we've covered, a playwright has the freedom to take his or her play in any direction, as long as it's logically true to his or her vision. Our fictitious play can end well, with Kirsten and Ashley standing up to the bully together and winning respect from new friends in their class. Yet plays don't have to always have happy endings—they should end sadly or tragically, if that fits the playwright's vision. If the audience or a critic doesn't appreciate a dark climax, that's OK, if that dark climax works for the established premise. A smart playwright always wants to be honest, but doesn't always need to be liked.

—————————SELECTED READINGS—————————

One-Acts vs. Full-Length Plays

The play's the thing—but it's not just ONE thing, at least when you're talking about the differences between a one-act and a full-length play. The two formats can be quite separate in terms of style, impact, and intention. Often, a playwright will choose to vividly express a single idea or theme by choosing one-act structure; if he or she wants to explore multiple themes within a story line, and expand character development significantly throughout a piece, then choosing a full-length structure makes the most sense.

Let's break down the unique characteristics of each format.

A one-act play:

- Generally has a fifteen-minute to one-hour running time.
- Focuses on one specific theme or situation.
- Has a streamlined plot that can still be creatively complex but that comes to some form of resolution without complicating subthemes.
- Most often, calls for only one setting.
- Consists of one long scene or a short string of brief scenes in a sequence.

Conversely, a full-length play:

- Runs on average from seventy minutes to over two hours.
- Is made up of two distinct acts, as we've covered.
- Can contain numerous settings.
- Consists of numerous scenes that can run from five to fifteen minutes or longer throughout both acts.
- Can accomplish a more layered, nuanced examination of theme through the text through its expanded length.

Interested in directing your first play, and want to choose the correct format for your skill level? Well, if you want to tackle a full-length play, by all means, go for it. You can learn a lot by thinking big and ambitiously taking on a long-form piece of material. Most first-time directors do tend to choose to try a one-act first, though. Why? With a smaller amount of material to interpret, you can really immerse yourself in the details of the play's story development, character meanings, and subtle points. Bottom line, don't be afraid to try helming either length—and don't shy away from writing your own play in either format, either (another stellar learning exercise).

A Critic's Perspective

Barry M. Willis is a highly experienced and highly respected theater critic, and he takes his job very seriously. A member of the American Theatre Critics Association and president of San Francisco Bay Area Theatre Critics Circle, Willis generously shares his thoughts on his career and the importance of the fair, intelligent analysis he employs every time he sits down to review a theater piece.

Q: Could you talk a bit about how you decided to become a theater critic? What experiences or influences started you on this journey?

A: I didn't actually decide to become a theater critic. It was sort of accidental. I had always enjoyed theater and other performing arts, and had worked as a journalist for many years in the high-performance audio/video field, work that sometimes included reviewing music, films, and TV shows. I also did sound design for the Angst Ensemble, a now defunct theater group in San Francisco. In 2001 my girlfriend was in a production of *Who's Afraid of Virginia Woolf?* In an attempt to generate some interest in the show, I wrote a review and sent it in to our local weekly newspaper. The editor got back to me immediately, saying, "I don't know who you are, but we can use you." That led to my doing regular reviews of theater events and visual arts—gallery openings, profiles of artists, that sort of thing. For the past ten years I have been one of two theater critics with the daily newspaper the *Marin Independent Journal*. I joined the San Francisco Bay Area Theatre Critics Circle about eight years ago and have been president of the group for the past five.

Q: How do you, as a critic, specifically evaluate the text of a play for quality, analyzing it separately from other elements of a production you're reviewing?

A: I don't read scripts unless I am helping an actor friend run lines. Contrary to what high school English teachers taught us, I don't think that plays are intended to be read as literature. They are blueprints for four-dimensional productions, that sometimes rise to the level of good literature. I do pay close attention to dialogue—does it sound plausible (not necessarily realistic), does it help propel the plot? The dialogue in many older productions—Shakespeare, Molière, Shaw, Chekhov, Wilde—is quite ornate and can be difficult for a contemporary audience. I appreciate the theatrical canon but prefer the work of contemporary playwrights, especially the new generation of women like Theresa Rebeck, Lynn Nottage, and Annie Baker.

Q: Any tips for students new to the experience of watching a play in terms of how to critically think about and evaluate the performance they are viewing? Are there any questions you can ask yourself while viewing a production to understand the performance more clearly and/or get more out of the theatrical experience as an audience member?

A: Rather than engaging in an internal dialogue about what is happening onstage, it's best to simply be there with the production and be as fully plugged in to it as you can be. If this is easy, and you get lost in the show, then that show is a success. You can pick it apart after the fact. I try to avoid reading any preshow publicity, including the notes in the playbill, because I want to have my own experience. I can read all of that later, including doing online research about the playwright or the history of the production. I don't want to have any assumptions or expectations. It's easy to do this with a new production and hard to do with a warhorse. I have seen fourteen productions of *Hamlet* and I am pretty sure that I know how it's going to start and how it's going to end. For the older stuff—Chekhov, Shaw, Molière, etc.—you probably need to prepare with some background information. In my reviews of Shakespeare, I usually devote a couple of paragraphs up front to explaining the plot. This is for the benefit of first-time theatergoers who may not know the stories and don't understand the language.

Q: What has been your most rewarding experience or experiences thus far as a critic? When and how did your work truly enrich or change your perspective?

A: Getting elected to the presidency of the San Francisco Bay Area Theatre Critics Circle has been a very rewarding experience. (Also a vexing one, in some ways.) Every spring we have a big awards ceremony in an old theater in San Francisco, honoring the previous year's best in eighty-some categories of performance, production, and technical excellence. It's a big, rowdy event with hundreds of attendees from throughout the theater community. It's incredibly gratifying that they appreciate our efforts as critics the same way we appreciate theirs as theater professionals.

How *Hamilton* Changed the Game

Hamilton: An American Musical by Lin-Manuel Miranda with Jeremy McCarter, based on the 2004 biography *Alexander Hamilton* by Ron Chernow, arguably changed the face of theater when it premiered in 2015. Why? *Hamilton*'s audacious, lively score is so exciting, accessible, and unforgettable that it opened up the musical theater art form to audiences who had never seen it before, and its engaging, whip-smart book got nonhistory buffs hooked on past political events. Quite a pair of accomplishments. And these were not the show's only remarkable achievements: *Hamilton* won eleven 2016 Tony awards, including Best Musical; the 2016 Pulitzer Prize for drama; eight Drama Desk Awards; and a Grammy Award for Best Musical Theater Album.

The show's birth came pretty much out of the blue. Miranda was killing time at the airport when he picked up a copy of Chernow's book and got so engrossed that he had a brainstorm it would make a great musical. Miranda's well-respected Broadway work already encompassed the award-winning musical *In the Heights*; he saw *Hamilton* as a story that could successfully be told through a mix of contemporary melody like rhythm and blues, pop and hip-hop, and a more traditional show-tune format. This would be the perfect recipe that would update the dramatic and compelling story of Alexander Hamilton's extraordinary life, from his personal interactions with his wife to his fatal duel with archenemy Aaron Burr. Miranda started writing his ideas for the musical almost immediately, coming up with the show's first version, titled *The Hamilton Mixtape*. Invited by President Barack Obama to the White House in 2009, Miranda performed the first song the world ever heard from the show, "Alexander Hamilton," in rough form; it garnered a big, enthusiastic response.

Miranda kept developing the show over the next four years; in July 2013, he presented it in workshop form at the Vassar College Reading Festival. Off-Broadway beckoned next—director Thomas Kail was brought in to stage the show, and it premiered at the Public Theater in February 2015 to across-the-board positive reviews and sellout crowds. The show transferred to the Richard Rodgers Theatre on Broadway in August 2015, where it's earned its right as a classic and a mainstay. Touring productions across the US and to the West End in London are further bringing *Hamilton*'s message to the masses.

So why should *Hamilton* matter to you? Three good reasons: (1) it's beyond entertaining, and the world (and you) always need that; (2) it humanizes historical figures in a way that makes them so compelling that you root for them, hate them, and/or understand them so much better than you ever could from a dry history text; and (3) it's a perfect illustration of how clear, concise writing meshes with clear, concise music to create a universally understood theater piece. It's a creative perfect storm, and it will inspire you to no end.

WORKSHEET ASSIGNMENT

Write a scene! Dive right in, using the guidelines you've learned throughout this chapter, and express yourself freely. Don't censor yourself—it's OK to make mistakes your first time out. A two-person scene is a great way to start. After you've completed a draft, ask two classmates to read your scene aloud. Do the setting and premise work? Does your dialogue sound natural? Note whatever you feel you could do better, do a bit of rewriting, and listen to your scene read aloud again. Rinse and repeat until you're satisfied with the finished product.

─────── **CHAPTER 3 CHECKLIST** ───────

Get more out of what you've learned in this chapter by:

☐ Listening to the *Hamilton* cast album. The first Broadway soundtrack to hit number one on Billboard's Rap Albums Chart, the album perfectly lays out the play's text in song, from soaring ballads to thrilling beats to swinging dancehall tunes. Losing yourself in this soundscape is a great way to truly understand the flow of *Hamilton*'s script.

☐ Writing a review of a play. Want to improve your critical thinking about what works, and what doesn't, in a theatrical context? Go to a student or professional production with pad and pen in hand. As Barry Willis so wisely advised, just stay plugged in to the play. Don't suppress any impression you have as right or wrong— criticism is the very definition of subjectivity. Let your opinions develop, and note them as they do. Jot down your thoughts about the story, characters, dialogue, actors, direction, everything you feel strongly about. Then, once you head home, assemble your review in prose form—check out a few great examples on how to do this by reading a few of Ben Brantley's terrific reviews in the *New York Times* (www.nytimes.com). Be generous in your praise, fair in your criticisms, and, most of all, true to your gut—and you'll *really* start to get the power of text.

4

All about Acting

Statistically, the vast majority of students who enroll in theater arts courses are interested primarily in acting—sound familiar to you? Yep, you're probably reading this book because your desire to perform has led you to want to absorb as much overall theatrical background information as possible—and that's a wise thing. But let's say your affinity is for directing, design, writing, or tech. Did you know it still benefits you to learn as much about acting as you can? It's true—arguably, acting is the lifeblood of the theater, the vessel through which all other meaningful work flows and is expressed to the audience. In short, it's the most obvious mode of theatrical communication.

This chapter focuses on the craft of acting, and the companion skills that make up an actor's tool kit. Now, it's very important to understand from the get-go that the craft of acting, specifically in terms of creative interpretation, is highly subjective. When it comes to best conveying the circumstances and identity of a character, the style and discipline that works best for one actor might not work at all for his cast mate. The number one universal truth about acting is do what feels right. That holds true for the technique you might choose to study, the decisions you make for your character from reading a play's text or writing out your character's background as a preparation tool, or interacting with your fellow actor in a scene. Good actors trust themselves and trust their instincts.

All actors have a toolbox—the essential elements they use in order to make their character's essence and intentions clear. The tools actors use work as follows:

THE ACTOR'S BODY

Your physical form is everything, of course. How do you best use your body fully to convey a character, in terms of movement and visual traits the audience can garner information from (like a limp, certain hand gestures, any and every kind of distinctive motions)? How does your voice help you as a key component—does your character have an accent; a lisp; a loud, booming delivery; or a shy, whispery tone?

Actors must first learn to feel free when it comes to using their bodies for the purpose of slipping into a new persona with ease. To this end, actors work very hard to "train" away stiffness, nervousness, and a sense of inhibition. At the start of an actor's training, relaxation exercises go a long way to help loosen up an actor's body. The study of voice/speech and movement/dance are also common ways new actors learn to harness the power of these elements of their bodies and utilize them as strengths when it comes to creating a character. Basically, an actor's goal is to feel physically liberated enough to be able to comfortably adopt any movement, trait, or affectation that's physically pertinent to any character they set out to play.

THE ACTOR'S TECHNIQUE

Next, there's the technical style an actor chooses in which to build a character from text to stage performance. Acting may seem pretty simple from the outside—lots of people think it's little more than pretending, as we all did for fun as kids. On the inside, though, the truth's much more complicated. Actors can choose to study a variety of highly developed performance philosophies, depending on what feels most comfortable and effective in terms of helping them break down the intentions, desires, and motivations of a character.

An actor will start building a character by reading through a script and will most often define, through notes and analysis, what his or her character's goals are throughout each scene, and, to a greater extent, throughout the entire play. Once an actor has established these "wants" or "needs" clearly, he or she will then often use a preferred performance technique to create the organic, yet strategic, progression of his or her character's personality, with a view toward clearly demonstrating how the character achieves these goals.

So which techniques are considered the most useful? Actors tend to feel pretty passionate about the style they feel works best for them personally. Here's a breakdown of several popular and diverse acting techniques/disciplines:

Classical Acting

Basically, classical acting is a pretty wide-ranging discipline; it encompasses the use of all aspects of an actor's physical and emotional strengths, such as use of the body, voice, and imagination. Developed primarily by acting guru Konstantin Stanislavski, classical acting also uses improvisation, personalization, and intense script study. Actors are encouraged to find common psychological ground between themselves and a character in this technique.

Method Acting

Method acting is probably the most widely used technique around the world today. Developed by legendary teacher Lee Strasberg (about whom you'll read more a little later in this chapter), the Method stresses the importance of using one's own life experiences to inform a character's actions. For example, the Method involves the extensive use of sense memory, a kind of emotional recall of a specific sound, sight, or smell within a real experience that the actor can use to make his/her character's experience feel authentic.

Meisner

The Meisner technique, developed by acting coach Sanford Meisner, requires an actor to maintain an intense focus on his or her scene partner; the relationship this creates onstage is used as the basis of character development for both actors, and subsequently informs the scene itself. It's considered an "external" technique, as opposed to drawing mainly from oneself to define a character's actions.

Practical Aesthetics

Lauded stage actor William H. Macy teamed with playwright David Mamet to create this most recent form of respected technique. With Practical Aesthetics, an actor uses four steps to work out his character's place in a scene: the literal circumstances of the scene itself; the "want," or what the actor is trying to get from other actors in the scene; the "essential action" of a scene, which is specific to the actor understanding what to do to get what he or she wants; and "as if," or relating the scene to a given experience from the actor's personal life. On the whole, Practical Aesthetics requires the actor to examine him- or herself, in order to use what he or she would do, instead of what the character would do.

No Set Technique at All

Many actors say they don't follow any special technique and basically see what happens when they show up to rehearsal. These actors are usually highly intuitive, confident, and very open to direction. Their process works best when they collaborate closely with a show's director on the direction of their character and when they experiment with the other actors they work with.

IMPROVISATION: A POWERFUL ACTING RESOURCE

To this end, improvisation, or as it's more commonly called in the theater, "improv," is an immensely important skill for an actor to learn, especially when that actor is experimenting with other performers. Improv, simply defined, is the spontaneous creation of a performance, literally made up as the actors doing it go along, with no set script (although often within the confines of a premise everyone in the scene understands). There is no better way for an actor to learn to think on his or her feet and stretch his or her imagination to the limit in terms of learning to tell a vivid story.

It's thought that improv was first used in performance in Africa, around 391 BC. Commedia dell'arte incorporated improv in many of its performances early on; later, Stanislavski reflected upon improv extensively when developing Method acting and trying to bring his new teaching form to its ultimate honesty. Early improv pioneers included Viola Spolin, who wrote the seminal book *Improvisation for the Theater*; Dudley Riggs, an inspired vaudeville actor; and Keith Johnstone, founder of the interactive performance troupe Theatresports. Paul Sills, who later founded the illustrious Second City comedy improv group in Chicago, began his work by creating the Compass Players, an extremely respected improv troupe (other influential improv troupes over time have included the Theatre Machine, the Groundlings, the Committee, and the Upright Citizens Brigade). Other lauded performers who got their starts excelling at improv include Elaine May, Eugene Levy, John Belushi, Tina Fey, Steve Carrell, and Stephen Colbert.

Performance elements of improv include the following:

- **Shortform**—brief vignettes improvised in situations suggested by the audience
- **The Harold**—a longer improv running a half hour or longer
- **The Cocktail Party**—a common scenario in which revolving improvised monologues happen

Crucial points actors practice during any solid improv include listening fully and intently to their partners' words; thinking for the good of the group in a scene, as opposed to stealing focus for him- or herself; always keeping the premise of the scene and one's character in mind; being willing to try something risky or interesting on the spot; and making choices constantly, with conviction, to move the scene in different, fascinating directions. Improv is fun for performers, of course, but when really well executed allows the audience to shape the action both by tossing out ideas to the actors and by reacting to what the actors do—raucous audience approval can often take a scene in a never-thought-of-this-before direction that allows for the most entertaining work!

OTHER KEY ELEMENTS ACTORS USE TO INTEGRATE THEIR PERFORMANCES INTO A FULL PRODUCTION

- **Input from a playwright,** if the work is original. Actors often call playwrights their "source"—who better to gain insight on their character from?
- **Backstory**. Actors often write extensive histories for their characters, creating childhood experiences, adult victories and disappointments, and personal qualities, in order to more clearly define the persona they're working to convey.
- **Reference materials**. Actors will often study the biographies of real-life characters they play or read up on the general circumstances of a fictional character's life to understand that character's psyche better.
- **Experience**. The more an actor acts, the more he or she understands about the mechanics of finding a character. Actors will stick with what the audience tells them works, too—a great payoff to a lot of tough, concentrated effort!

————SELECTED READINGS————

Here are profiles of three of the most talented, inventive, and brilliant actors ever to grace a stage.

The Architect of Acting: Laurence Olivier

Laurence Olivier's work as an actor was so groundbreaking, thrilling, and original, he arguably will be considered the world's greatest stage actor for ages to come. Regarded by other actors with total awe for his uniquely creative, deeply emotional interpretations of Shakespearean characters and other classic roles, Olivier possessed a ferocious and dedicated work ethic; he tirelessly innovated many aspects of acting theory and technique and influenced his onstage collaborators to do their best work as well.

Olivier was born on May 22, 1907, in Surrey in the UK. His father, a colorful clergyman, decided that the young Laurence showed an innate flair for the dramatic and encouraged his son's earliest acting ambitions. Olivier enrolled as a child at All Saints School in London, where he started performing in plays—at the mere age of ten, he delivered a tour de force as Julius Caesar. Moving on to St. Edward's School in Oxford, Olivier performed memorably as Puck in *A Midsummer Night's Dream*; his desire for more theater training cemented, he went on to the Central School of Speech Training and Dramatic Art. He swiftly applied what he learned there to his work as a touring company performer and became renowned for his incredible ability to decipher and interpret Shakespeare for audiences in a way that was easily understandable and profoundly moving.

In 1928, Olivier got his big break in the West End. Shortly after, he made his first film, *The Temporary Widow*, in 1930. This began a period of great upward trajectory in Olivier's career. Playwright Noël Coward saw his work and wanted him immediately cast in his play *Private Lives*; Olivier also scored an RKO Pictures deal. Olivier also started working with his friendly rival John Gielgud—the two appeared in a 1935 production of *Romeo and Juliet*, in which they switched in and out of the Romeo role, spurring them both on to do their individual best. Joining the Old Vic in 1936, Olivier began performing in a string of more Shakespearean works, from *Macbeth* to *Othello* to *Coriolanus*. He became known as a true shape-shifter as an actor, effortlessly mastering any number of accents and physical changes as needed in any given role and doing so with uncanny realism.

Olivier's presence truly began to dominate the film world in 1938, when he received a Best Actor Oscar nod for playing Heathcliff in *Wuthering Heights*. He worked for Alfred Hitchcock in *Rebecca* and also appeared in *Pride and Prejudice* before answering the call to serve his country, enlisting in the British Fleet Air Army during World War II. After the war, Olivier returned to the theater and the movies, diversifying his work by becoming codirector of the Old Vic, directing and starring in *Hamlet* (which earned him the Best Actor Oscar in 1947), and becoming a producer (he established Laurence Olivier Productions and took over the management of the St. James Theatre in London).

Olivier continued racking up brilliant performances onscreen (in *Richard III* and *Hamlet*) and accepted new leadership responsibilities in the theater community, with a view toward guiding actors and directors to produce their most emotional and daring work. He became the director of the National Theatre in the UK in 1961, directing its legendary first production of *Hamlet* with Peter O'Toole in the title role (he would remain as the institution's head for thirteen years). As the '60s passed into the '70s, Olivier reinvigorated his career once again, turning his attention back to film. He unleashed a fun star turn opposite Michael Caine in the mystery movie *Sleuth*, played a homicidal dentist in *Marathon Man*, and lit up the political thriller *The Boys from Brazil*.

Olivier also began working regularly on television, taking on *The World at War*, *Love among the Ruins*, and *Brideshead Revisited*. Even when his health began to fail, he kept working; after being diagnosed with the muscle disease dermatomyositis, Olivier turned in a stunning final stage performance as *King Lear* in 1983. He passed away from renal failure on July 11, 1989.

Olivier was married three times, to Jill Esmond, Vivien Leigh, and his widow Joan Plowright, often collaborating with his wives on film and onstage in memorable fashion. He garnered four Oscars and five Emmys and had his name forever honored with the West End's highest honor, the Olivier Award. His creative legacy is truly peerless. Seeking out his work on film is an absolute must-do for every theater student—expect to be moved, surprised, awed, and vastly entertained.

The Born Actress: Meryl Streep

Haunting . . . funny . . . chameleon-like . . . regal . . . fiercely intelligent. These are just a few of the adjectives that apply to arguably the world's greatest living stage and film actress, Meryl Streep. Streep's talent is completely natural and organic—it's been said she was simply born to be an actress. Yet her almost scholarly ability to vividly use her carefully built creative technique to inhabit a stunning array of characters never ceases to amaze audiences and critics. To this end, at this writing, Streep has earned twenty-one Oscar nominations, winning three times (Best Supporting Actress in 1979 for *Kramer vs. Kramer*, Best Actress in 1982 for *Sophie's Choice*, and Best Actress in 2011 for *The Iron Lady*), as well as racking up scores of additional honors, from the Emmy to the BAFTA and more.

She was born Mary Louise Streep on June 22, 1949, in Summit, New Jersey. As Streep grew up, she wasn't particularly interested in theater or film—she focused instead on being an excellent student and was also a popular high school cheerleader. The young Meryl diligently took singing lessons from childhood, but her astonishing talent as an actress didn't fully come to light until she auditioned for the lead role in *Miss Julie* while an undergraduate at Vassar College. Her stunning and fully formed performance while simply reading her lines became legendary, as Streep had almost no experience acting in any kind of serious material at that point in her life. She threw herself into learning the craft from that point forward, subsequently earning a coveted spot in Yale Drama School's graduate program. At Yale, Streep excelled at interpreting the early works of Christopher Durang and Albert Innaurato and was mentored by Yale's highly respected teacher Robert Brustein. During her university years, she also spent time expanding her educational horizons as a visiting student at Dartmouth College.

After years of applying herself academically, Streep dashed off to Manhattan immediately after receiving her Yale master of fine arts in 1975. Astoundingly, she got the first job she ever professionally auditioned for—a role in *Trelawny of the Wells* at Lincoln Center. Joe Papp, artistic director of New York City's revered Public Theater, quickly scooped her up, and she began working constantly for him via the New York Shakespeare Festival—she carved out one illuminating performance after another in productions such as *Henry V*, *The Taming of the Shrew*, and *Measure for Measure*. She lit up the Broadway stage in *Happy End*, *The Cherry Orchard*, *27 Wagons Full of Cotton*, and *A Memory of Two Mondays* and won an Obie Award for her Off-Broadway turn in *Alice at the Palace*. Streep also garnered an Emmy Award for her moving performance in the made-for-TV-movie *Holocaust*.

Then the silver screen came calling. Streep's first film role was a small turn in *Julia* in 1977, but her presence was instantly indelible, and offers for bigger parts started pouring in. She received her first Oscar nomination for *The Deer Hunter* in 1978 and then earned terrific reviews for *The Seduction of Joe Tynan* and *Manhattan* in 1979. Around this time in her life, Streep was flourishing professionally for sure, but personally, she was dealing with the untimely death of her great love and collaborator, actor John Cazale. They had worked together both onstage and in *The Deer Hunter*; prior to Cazale's death from lung cancer in 1978, Streep was also his devoted caregiver.

Once again focusing on her work, Streep's film career continued to skyrocket—she was cast in *Kramer vs. Kramer*, winning almost universal acclaim for her vulnerable, touching work as a young mother who gives up custody of her child. Her Academy Award for the film didn't alter her down-to-earth nature: at the ceremony in 1980, Streep charmingly forgot her Oscar in the ladies' room because she was so nervous and elated over her win. She went on to play such varied roles during this time as a mysterious femme fatale in *The French Lieutenant's Woman*, a doomed nuclear power plant worker in *Silkwood*, and, in her most celebrated part, a traumatized Holocaust survivor in *Sophie's Choice* in 1982. For *Sophie's Choice*, Streep perfected a Polish accent with incredible detail and so fully embodied the pain of her character that it almost became too difficult for many to watch her. The film's famous flashback scene in which her character is forced to choose which of her young children to give to a Nazi guard, ensuring the child's death, is widely recognized as one of the greatest pieces of acting ever committed to film; even the most technically experienced actors and directors say to this day that they could emotionally handle watching the scene only once.

Streep's streak of perfect portrayals continued throughout the 1980s, 1990s, and 2000s, in films including *Plenty, Out of Africa, Postcards from the Edge, The Bridges of Madison County, Adaptation, The Hours, The Devil Wears Prada, Doubt, August: Osage County,* and *Into the Woods.* Her work grew even more daring—she aced a challenging interpretation of chef Julia Child in *Julie & Julia*, belted out vintage ABBA tunes with relish in *Mamma Mia!*, and emerged victorious with a tough, illuminating take on British prime minster Margaret Thatcher in *The Iron Lady.* Streep also kept active in the New York theater community via her affecting work in the Public Theater productions of *The Seagull* (2001) and *Mother Courage and Her Children* (2006). She also scored a second Emmy for *Angels in America*, the moving television adaptation of Tony Kushner's socially significant stage masterpiece. Speaking of socially significant, Streep's that, too; she's been an outspoken proponent of liberal political causes, has supported the Equal Rights Amendment and the ONE Campaign, and funds scholarships plus screenwriting study for aspiring female filmmakers.

And to top of all of these accomplishments? Streep is a very proud mom. She and her husband, the respected sculptor Don Gummer, are the parents of Henry, Mamie, Grace, and Louisa—and her acting talent continues to flow into the next generation, as Mamie and Grace are gifted actresses in their own rights.

The Method Master: Lee Strasberg

Lee Strasberg's mark on the acting world is indelible. Known as the creative force behind Method acting—a stage performance technique that requires the use of real-life feelings and experiences to build a character—Strasberg's work as a teacher has shaped the talents of scores of the world's best thespians, including Al Pacino, Paul Newman, Geraldine Page, Marilyn Monroe, Jack Nicholson, Jane Fonda, Ellen Burstyn, Dustin Hoffman, Harvey Keitel, and Sally Field.

Strasberg was born Israel Strassberg on November 17, 1901, in what's now the Ukraine (he later changed his name for professional reasons). His family came to the United States, settling in New York City. As a young man, Strasberg was not very interested in traditional education, dropping out of high school. Instead he was drawn to performance, working first in Yiddish productions and then moving on to become a member of the Chrystie Street Settlement Houses's drama club. He did feel an affinity for theater studies; he started acting classes at the Clare Tree Major School of the Theater as well as the American Laboratory Theatre. Strasberg became fascinated by the performance philosophy of the great Russian acting teacher Stanislavski, after seeing a performance by the Moscow Art Theatre in 1923. To him, the very natural, seemingly spontaneous style of the company's actors, as Stanslavski had coached them, rang so true and organic he had to do something similar. Strasberg began working on a unique acting process that would utilize relaxation, memory, and recall of the senses, and as cofounder of the Group Theatre with Harold Clurman and Cheryl Crawford in 1931, began teaching this process, which would come to be called Method acting, or the Method.

The Method quickly became a demanding but highly effective and helpful technique for both aspiring and established actors alike. Strasberg was known as both a supportive and challenging instructor.

And he was nothing if not selective: when he became director of the Actors Studio in New York in 1951 (a Method mecca, which also had a branch in Los Angeles) only about five actors out of every thousand auditioners were accepted for classes. Strasberg's teaching agenda encompassed improvisation, personal discipline, creative honesty, and realism of technique. He also honed the now-common performance preparation technique of creating a backstory, or life story, for a character so an actor can draw upon this history when making choices in a scene.

Outside of the classroom, Strasberg was married three times, and had four children, including the acclaimed actress Susan Strasberg. He also practiced what he preached, appearing in six films throughout his teaching career. Most notably, and at the urging of Al Pacino, one of his most dedicated students, Strasberg accepted a role in 1974's *The Godfather Part II*, receiving an Oscar nomination for Best Supporting Actor. His intense, realistic performance in that film is the perfect example of the strength of the Method, which continues to aid and shape the skill sets of actors worldwide today.

——————WORKSHEET ASSIGNMENT——————

Write a review of one of Meryl Streep's stage-to-screen film performances—the film adaptation of David Hare's *Plenty* is a great piece to choose. Discuss in-depth how Streep makes her character ring so true, in terms of how she uses her body and voice specifically to inhabit the role.

──────── CHAPTER 4 CHECKLIST ────────

Get more out of what you've learned in this chapter by:

☐ Reading *Respect for Acting* by Uta Hagen (Wiley Publishing). First released in 1973, this is the actor's bible, as written by one of the world's great acting coaches and dramatic thinkers. Hagen emphasizes the importance of problem solving for actors first and foremost in the book and focuses strongly on using the individual performer's instincts as a way to reveal a character's true being. Fascinating and very useful.

☐ Auditing a skill class like voice or movement. Get a firsthand feel for how actors hone their physical powers by trying out a class for a day. Sing, stretch, jump, shout—see how freeing and fun getting in touch with your instrument truly feels.

☐ Watching *Curb Your Enthusiasm*. This long-running, hilarious sitcom is completely made up on the spot, with just a simple set premise for each scene within each episode—the perfect illustration of expert improvisation. Series stars Larry David, Jeff Garlin, Susie Essman, Cheryl Hines, and J. B. Smoove, plus a plethora of guest stars, including Ted Danson and Richard Lewis, are masters at making scenes appear completely realistic *and* off-the-cuff; check them out and learn by osmosis.

5

All about Directing

The director of a play is the boss; this you already know. Still, you might not be aware of the incredibly varied and nuanced talent it takes to direct a show effectively. A director is a lot more than that person who just tells other people where to stand onstage. Nope, an efficient director must also be a perfect planner with an artistic eye, a yen for collaboration, a knack for tactful diplomacy, a technical mind-set, and, best-case scenario, a lack of ego. These qualities help a director helm a production from start to finish with a clear head and with his or her smarts firing on all cylinders.

Here's a comprehensive examination of the craft of directing, from both an artistic and a technical expertise perspective. Let's break down the tasks every director must complete at each stage of his or her work so that the play that results ends up being a high-quality, sensible, artistically meaningful piece. The work a director must undertake in this regard is detailed, tough, exhausting, and taxing, but, ultimately, very rewarding if committed to fully and properly—and the audience always lets a director know if the effort has paid off.

SETTLING UPON A VITAL VISION

The enemy of any play production is indecision. A director, before doing anything else, must determine what he or she wants to say in terms of interpreting the material presented and stick to that concept. What is the theme or message that will be the driving force of the production's action? What visual style will the play have? What kind of technical stagecraft will be utilized to make the production's over-all statements clear to the audience? The director needs to know these things, because if he or she is feeling self-conscious or unsure, or just figures everything can be made up as rehearsals merrily roll along, the play is doomed. Clarity is a director's best friend.

OK, so maybe every choice a director settles on won't be the perfect option, but it's key to take a firm position anyway. This pays off in so many ways: because a director's overall intent shapes a production in every aspect, the cast, designers, and crew will automatically have a road map for their own work from the get-go, which builds creativity and confidence. And sure, sometimes a director will discover that the perspective the production is going forth with has its flaws as the work unfolds—most likely, that will happen for sure. Adjustments can be made if needed, of course. Rarely, though, will a director regret an overall point of view for a production, if he or she has taken the time to think it through carefully, made extensive notes working out the bugs in this concept, and gotten feedback from the rest of the play's team—all that preparation pays off.

A good director will formulate his or her vision for a production by, first and foremost, reading the play to be staged many times, till it's known like the back of one's hand. Directors, as mentioned before, always take lots of notes—this process is essential for understanding the material being undertaken, asking important questions, and recording key impressions and ideas so everything will mesh into one cohesive intent. A director should also realistically evaluate how his or her intent can be achieved from a practical standpoint. Will the space the play will be presented in work in terms of the size of certain effects? Does the budget allotted for a production mean this play can be done right, without looking cheap? These considerations should always be dealt with, and any problems worked out, before moving on to assembling a production team.

WORKING WITH A DESIGN TEAM

A director's next step is to choose a lighting designer, a costume designer, a set designer, and possibly a sound designer and projection designer. Each of these key production team members should be an individual the director respects creatively, and who the director feels will be skilled and competent in terms of realizing the play's visual and technical potential. Trust here is very key. The director should be able to explain what he or she wants, know each team member understands this goal completely, and then feel comfortable letting each designer fly, knowing their best work will follow.

A good director isn't a micromanager; rather, he or she allows his or her team the freedom to try things, make mistakes, and start again. The best way to accomplish this is to hold on loosely; a good director makes a point of checking in on a regular basis with each designer, keeps the lines of communication open, and allows problems, changes, and questions to be addressed before they become bigger issues.

CHOOSING A STAGE MANAGER

The stage manager is the director's eyes, ears, hands, and feet. A smart, resourceful SM will be able to put out technical fires, handle the day-to-day work supervision of each member of the production, carry out the director's wishes creatively and efficiently, and remember everything. Many directors work early on with a stage manager they click with and then hire that SM again and again—always a fruitful opportunity if you can grab it.

CHOOSING A CAST

A director's next job is to choose the right actors for each role in the play. This is done, of course, through the audition process. Usually, the director will ask each actor to do a monologue; if the actor does well and seems like a possible fit for a particular part or parts, the director will "call back" that actor. Usually, a callback consists of having the actor read a scene from the play itself, often with other actors the director is considering, to test for chemistry. A director will also sometimes give some specific instructions to an actor during a callback to test the actor's instincts and see if that actor is easy to work with.

In making the final decision as to whether to cast an actor, a wise director will weigh such factors as the actor's talent, training, vocal ability, physical appearance as it fits a particular character in the play, knack for taking direction, and overall professionalism. Then, the director assembles the cast, pairing all of the performers he or she likes with the appropriate roles.

BLOCKING AND OTHER STAGING WORK

A director is responsible for every move his or her actors make onstage. This is accomplished via meticulous preplanning; the director makes blocking notes in the script going line by line, so actors walk, sit, or shift stage positions at set points in each scene. Often, a director will work with an actor to make sure the blocking feels right in terms of the actor's choices for a character.

A director will also know every point of the set's layout, so he or she can use it to best advantage when moving action from one place to the other onstage. Some directors incorporate the entire house into their staging, allowing actors to enter or exit from the audience, or on flies—really, the sky can be the limit in terms of a director's imagination and ingenuity.

GIVING CONSTRUCTIVE CRITICISM

A director must guide actors, designers, and crew through insightful input and useful feedback throughout the production process. Directors often meet one-on-one with actors to work on the backstory of their characters' lives and give advice and reminders on a daily basis as the actors hone their approach in rehearsal. A director will watch an actor's scene or monologue work to make sure the actor's goals and intentions are coming across, to help the actor pace his or her performance, and to make sure the material itself is clear and authentic as interpreted. The director will also give his or her opinion liberally to designers as their work fully forms and will consistently work with the stage manager to make sure all the technical requirements are being met by crew members on the show. To this end, the director helms all technical and dress rehearsals to work out all the show's final kinks before opening.

Directors give notes throughout the entire production process— these notes should always be full of constructive criticism (although some directors can go overboard and get snarky, or complain too much—not helpful or humane). The value of offering solutions, not grievances, through notes can't be overstated. After all, it's the director's job to solve problems *with* his or her personnel, not to blame them. A democratic, diplomatic delivery of criticism, coupled with ideas and dialogue regarding ideas to fix things, is always the way to go.

KNOWING WHEN THE JOB IS DONE

A director attends opening night of his or her production, of course— but after that doesn't really do a lot of tweaking. Of course, a good director will always monitor a show's run to give notes when a glaring issue needs to be corrected and will often direct new cast members to be put in during a long run. But once the show is up, a good director knows his or her work is finished—the play is its own entity, and it belongs to those who see it. Giving a play away to the world, most directors agree, feels like a pretty neat achievement.

SELECTED READINGS

Here are three profiles of three of the most exciting, daring, and brilliant theater directors who have worked in modern theater.

The Classic Chameleon: Mike Nichols

Mike Nichols reigned for decades as one of theater and film's most brilliant directors, building a hugely diverse body of work that broke cultural barriers and always expressed significant themes. Nichols directed on Broadway from the 1960s to the 2000s; his productions included *The Odd Couple*, *The Knack*, *St. Joan*, *Comedians*, *Luv*, *Players*, *The Importance of Being Earnest*, *Monty Python's Spamalot*, *Plaza Suite*, *The Apple Tree*, *The Little Foxes*, *Streamers*, *The Prisoner of Second Avenue*, *Uncle Vanya*, *The Gin Game*, *The Real Thing*, *Hurlyburly*, *Waiting for Godot*, *Death of a Salesman*, and *Betrayal*. He also made an incredible mark in film, directing *The Graduate* (for which he received the Best Director Oscar), *Carnal Knowledge*, *Catch-22*, *Who's Afraid of Virginia Woolf?*, *Silkwood*, *Working Girl*, and *Closer*, among other respected works.

Born Mikhail Igor Peschkowsky in November 1931 in Berlin, Germany, he fled the Nazi invasion as a child to join his father, who became a doctor in New York City. Nichols was a good student and planned on becoming a doctor as well; he attended New York University and was about to enroll in the premed program at the University of Chicago when, as a fluke, he got work as a performer on a radio show in the Windy City. Nichols found he loved acting, started doing plays, and one night spied a young woman attentively watching him from the front row while he was onstage. She was writer/comedienne Elaine May, who would become his trusted theatrical performance partner and lifelong friend. After Nichols went back to New York briefly to study with Lee Strasberg, he was drawn back to the Chicago comedy scene. After working with both the Compass Players and Second City, he and May decided to focus on working as a comedy duo. Their wry, smart style earned them acclaim on Broadway (in *An Evening with Nichols and May*), and they influenced a generation of comedic hopefuls before their professional split in 1961. (Years later, they decided to work together again, and May wrote the screenplays for his films *Primary Colors* and *The Birdcage*).

Nichols had a strong interest in directing, and quickly sought out stage work. His first production of note was *Barefoot in the Park*, starring a young Robert Redford, in 1963. The critics immediately embraced his deceptively easy but multilayered directing style. Throughout his career, Nichols garnered a reputation as an extremely thorough director, paying attention to every last detail of every production himself—he was known for personally directing every replacement actor who stepped into his famously long-running shows.

Known for his warm rapport with actors, many of whom worked with him over and over again, Nichols championed the stage careers of respected film stars like Daniel Craig and Natalie Portman, in addition to working with legends from Meryl Streep to Dustin Hoffman to Jessica Tandy to Philip Seymour Hoffman. Nichols also believed in nurturing the next generation of performers—to this end, he cofounded the New Actors Workshop training program and theater, often lecturing there. He also made his mark in television, directing a groundbreaking adaptation of the classic play *Angels in America*.

Nichols was married four times, lastly to television journalist Diane Sawyer. He passed away in November 2014 of a heart attack, saddening his family, friends, collaborators, and fans. Yet his excellent work lives on and serves as a great illumination on both the human spirit and perceptive artistic technique.

The Great Communicator: Joe Mantello

One of the best contemporary directors working today, as well as a working actor, Joe Mantello's skills span memorable contemporary premieres (often in collaboration with today's best playwrights) as well as the classics. An actor's director, Mantello's unique bond and vibe with his performers creates the best work time and again; he's known for his ability to communicate extremely effectively, speaking his actors' creative language in a fluent, reassuring way.

Joseph Mantello was born on December 27, 1962, in Rockford, Illinois. His early interest in theater spurred him on to study at the North Carolina School of the Arts. From the start of his professional career, Mantello valued collaboration with artists who shared his honest, humane approach to dramatic storytelling. To this end, he founded the Edge Theater with M. L. Smith and Peter Hedges and became a member of the revered Naked Angels and Roundabout Theatre companies after moving to New York. Mantello first found acclaim as an actor; among his early roles was a lauded turn in *The Baltimore Waltz* by playwright Paula Vogel.

Mantello went on to receive a Tony nomination as Louis in the Broadway masterpiece *Angels in America*. His concurrent interest in directing led him to seek out plays to interpret that were very eclectic and varied in style. Mantello quickly began racking up New York directing credits, including *Frankie and Johnny in the Clair De Lune*, *The Santaland Diaries*, *The Vagina Monologues*, *Love! Valour! Compassion!*, *Other Desert Cities*, *Wicked*, *Take Me Out* (for which he won the 2003 Tony Award for Best Direction of a Play), and *Assassins* (for which he won the 2004 Tony award for Best Direction of a Play). He also earned two Drama Desk Awards and developed close and artistically significant bonds with Broadway's best playwrights, including Terrence McNally and his former partner Jon Robin Baitz.

Mantello continues to work as a stage actor on Broadway; he received his second Tony nomination as a performer for the revival of *The Normal Heart* in 2011 and starred opposite Sally Field in the 2017 reboot of *The Glass Menagerie*. His ability to move back and forth effortlessly between modern pieces and classic material, in addition to the empathetic shorthand he employs while directing actors, has assured his spot in theatrical history already and will make his work fascinating to watch for years to come.

The Vivid Visionary: Julie Taymor

Julie Taymor is an artistic force of nature, whose original imprint on a production is always breathtaking, thrilling, and moving to audiences. The director of Broadway's genius rethinking of *The Lion King* (1997), Taymor develops productions that are breathtaking to watch, stir the deepest of emotions, and have an avant-garde philosophy that helps theatergoers understand the importance of accepting new artistic concepts. Taymor became the first woman to win the Tony award for Best Direction of a Musical and is known for her fierce intelligence and commitment to her theatrical philosophy.

Taymor was born on December 15, 1952, in Newton, Massachusetts, and from the start was both an academic and dramatic prodigy. She started acting at age ten with the Boston Children's Theatre; graduating from high school early at sixteen, she immediately moved to Paris, her sights set on studying mime and mask. Taymor began working there with the highly esteemed L'École Internationale de Théâtre Jacques Lecoq, working toward her undergraduate degree at Oberlin College by correspondence course at the same time. She subsequently earned a Watson Fellowship, using it to explore theatrical art forms in Japan and Indonesia in the 1970s, and founded the dance/mask company Teatr Loh. She also pushed herself further as an actor by working with experimental theater greats like Joseph Chaikin.

Taymor met musician/composer Elliot Goldenthal in 1980; he became both her life partner and valued creative collaborator. Back in the US, she staged an admired production of *A Midsummer Night's Dream* at the Public Theater in 1984, then another acclaimed production, *The Tempest*, at Theatre for a New Audience in 1986. In 1991, she was awarded both a Guggenheim Fellowship and a MacArthur Fellowship, both tremendously prestigious honors. On Broadway, Taymor made her mark by directing an acclaimed production of *The Green Bird* before taking on *The Lion King*. Her take on the material that Disney had made famous onscreen was a beautiful whirlwind of bigger-than-life masked costumes, simple yet impactful staging, and a graceful interpretation of the beloved story's themes. Taymor also designed the show's costumes, earning an additional Tony for this remarkable effort.

Taymor went on to develop and direct *Spiderman: Turn Off the Dark* in 2011, an ambitious, unconventional take on the comic book premise that became very controversial; she became embroiled in disagreement with the show's producers, and ultimately the production closed before meeting the expectations of all involved. Her brilliant work continues to make inroads in several art forms.

Taymor has branched out into film, directing *Frida, Across the Universe, The Tempest*, and *Titus Andronicus*; she's also directed numerous operas, including *The Flying Dutchman* and *Oedipus Rex*. Additional honors Taymor has earned include an Emmy, an Oscar nomination for original song, the Brandeis University Creative Arts Award, and the Dorothy B. Chandler Award in Theatre. It will be thrilling to see where her huge imagination takes us all next.

WORKSHEET ASSIGNMENT

Go to YouTube and choose to watch one dramatic scene from the Broadway show of your choice, any era. Write an analysis of what you think the director did specifically in this scene to help guide the actors' motivations, based on the choices and conflicts they are playing out. Of course, you can't know the specifics of exactly how the scene was directed; that's OK. What you want to try to do instead is get a sense of how the director *may* have heightened the scene's conflict by encouraging the actors to demonstrate certain intent and emotion. It's your personal creative opinion. End your analysis by noting how you, as a director, might have directed the actors differently in theory.

───────── CHAPTER 5 CHECKLIST ─────────

Get more out of what you've learned in this chapter by:

☐ Watching *Who's Afraid of Virginia Woolf?* A terrific
adaptation (by screenwriter Ernest Lehman) of Edward
Albee's stage play, this 1966 film was directed with power
and wit by Mike Nichols. A great example of a director
allowing his actors great freedom with building stellar
characters. Elizabeth Taylor, Richard Burton, George Segal,
and Sandy Dennis truly deliver in this regard, and Nichols
creates a brash, funny, shocking creative statement overall.

☐ Reading *A Director Prepares: Seven Essays on Art and
Theatre* by Anne Bogart (published by Routledge). Bogart,
an iconic experimental stage director, discusses the art
form of directing from the unique standpoint of analyzing
seven emotional premises—violence, memory, terror,
eroticism, stereotype, embarrassment, and resistance. Her
contention is that each of these emotional premises is an
obstacle that can block a director from accessing the true
essence of a play. A fascinating, mind-changing take.

☐ Directing a monologue. Pair up with a classmate,
choose a monologue together (*Dramatic Monologues: a
Contemporary Anthology* By Samuel Maio, published by
the University of Evansville Press, has a great selection of
poems to get you started), and guide your actor through
the delivery of his or her speech. Decide what the character
your actor is playing wants, and make sure this goal is clear.
Help the actor keep the emotion in the monologue honest.
Keep your staging extremely simple—just have your actor
sit or stand at center stage—and focus on the truth of the
words. When you both feel ready, perform the piece for
your class, and ask for feedback—no doubt you'll learn a lot.

6

All about
Playwrighting

If it ain't on the page, it ain't on the stage—you've probably heard this pearl of wisdom before. And it's completely true—without a well-crafted, intelligent, meaningful piece of source material, a show is really built on hot air, no matter how dazzling its production design is or brilliantly talented its actors might be. The real heroes of every terrific theatrical experience you have, as a participant or even just an audience member, are the writers who bring the production's premise and words to vivid life in the first place.

Let's talk about playwrighting in depth. In learning how, precisely, a writer's choices influence every other aspect of a theatrical production at every stage of its development, we need to understand the primary elements that writer must determine as he or she plans, then executes, a theatrical idea.

A playwright's essential tasks encompass the following.

CHOOSING A TOPIC THAT IS VISUALLY RIGHT FOR THE THEATER, AS OPPOSED TO OTHER MEDIA

Theater is an art form that shouldn't be restrictive for its artists in any way. Yet you will hear theater teachers and critics talk about which subjects best fit a theatrical format, as opposed, say, to a different format such as a short story, novel, or screenplay. In reality, though, this contention is unnecessarily limiting. A writer should be able to explore any topic he or she wishes to within a play structure—all it takes is using a little imagination, so you have room within a one- or two-act structure to make room for everything you want to say.

Here's an example: let's say you want to write a comedy about every single US president there has ever been. A one-act. Sounds crazy-making impossible, doesn't it? You can do it if you get creative. Start off by creating a narrator explaining that your play is "presidential in a nutshell." Then, you can boil down the facts of each president's life into a colorful, clever, funny poem/monologue performed by that president. Since, at this writing, there have been forty-five presidents of the US in total, you might think, how will I practically suggest casting forty-five actors to play each one individually? No need to. You can shoot for a quick amount of stage time for each president, George Washington to Donald Trump—one minute apiece. Suggest on your cast page that between ten and twelve actors can play multiple roles. Voilà—you've just provided your future audiences with the ultimate speedy history lesson, in a fresh and highly entertaining way.

This example teaches a great golden rule about theater in general: anything is possible. Where there's a will, there's a way. If you want to make something happen onstage, just make it happen.

UTILIZING THEMES IN THE WRITING OF A PLAY

Most often, a playwright intends his or her play to be about a greater good (or bad, as the case may be). Think about a well-known piece like *West Side Story*: on a basic level, it's a doomed tale of love be-tween Tony and Maria, but in the greater scheme of things, it's also a strong commentary on how divisions in society lead to violence and destruction.

Choosing the right theme for a play is a balancing act. You don't want your theme to be so glaringly obvious that you're hitting your audience over the head with it through every character's words or actions. Yet you don't want your theme to feel obscure or be so hidden that no one gets the larger point you're making at all. The way a smart playwright solves this problem is by keeping his or her theme simple and logical—that equates to complete clarity. Want to say something significant about the importance of equal pay for women? Focus your story line on a working mom who stands up to a discriminatory boss—and wins.

It can be tempting to try to insert multiple themes into a play, but it most often muddies the waters. A wise writer just picks one overrid-ing thought, then doesn't stress too much about it—he or she just lets the story and characters develop organically from that point forward. That way the theme is always present but isn't forced or obvious.

CRAFTING DIALOGUE

Writing a good conversation can seem to be quite a challenge, but in actuality, to do it well, all you have to do is listen.

Paying attention to the way people in real life express themselves, and being able to determine the differences in how individual people speak, is really the whole battle. Many playwrights are said to have a natural ear for how people speak naturally, and that can be true—if you're a native New Yorker, sure, you're going to understand innately how a cab driver from Brooklyn might deliver a sentence. Yet there are some easy and highly effective tricks every playwright can use to craft authentic dialogue:

- Using the rhythm of normal speech. People don't speak like robots—they say "um" and "uh" a lot. It's OK to write dialogue like this, if it fits a specific character.

- Not being super declarative. In real life, people often talk *around* what they want to say rather than always coming right out and saying it immediately. A scene between two prospective love interests is much more true to life, and interesting, if flirtatious dialogue comes before one character tells the other, "I'd like to go out with you." Subtle dialogue choices build dramatic tension and interest.
- Reading every piece of dialogue back to themselves and asking the simple question, "Do people really talk like this?" The immediate answer that springs to mind tells a playwright if he or she has accomplished the goal at hand. If not, it's time to do a little more real-life listening before going back to the drawing board.

WRITING AN ORIGINAL PLAY AS OPPOSED TO AN ADAPTATION

An adaptation of a book, story, or film can be a very interesting exercise for a playwright to undertake. Of course, care has to be taken to remain true to the source material being adapted, first and foremost. Usually, a playwright will be rightfully respectful of the essence of the established story line and characters. Liberties can be taken, though, in terms of writing in visual elements that can push the material forward in a dramatic fashion. Changes such as reordering points in the story or cutting or creating a new character or two sometimes can work well, too.

Yet a good playwright knows this: he or she wouldn't be interested in adapting a great work if it was going to change *too* much. If you want to expand on the idea of a previously existing work, try an entirely different take on the idea, in an entirely brand-new play. A terrific example of how a gifted playwright can achieve this would be Lucas Hnath's excellent play *A Doll's House, Part 2*, a sequel to Ibsen's classic that reimagines and expands upon the original play's iconic characters' fates.

THE PLAYWRIGHT'S ROLE IN A PRODUCTION AS IT PREPARES TO GO UP

A playwright, when at all possible, should be available to a director and actors during the rehearsal process to answer questions, make changes he or she agrees with, and provide overall guidance whenever it's requested or whenever the playwright feels it's appropriate. The end result of this kind of effort will always be the best result.

A PLAYWRIGHT'S POINT OF VIEW: MERIDITH FRIEDMAN

Playwright Meridith Friedman has established herself as an illuminating theatrical voice. She received her bachelor of arts from Connecticut College, and her master of fine arts from Northwestern University. Her writing has been produced, developed, and workshopped at theaters and festivals across the country, including Curious Theatre Company, Kitchen Dog Theater, Stage Left Theatre, LOCAL Theatre Company, Chicago's Theatre on the Lake, Actor's Theater of Charlotte, the Kennedy Center, Chicago Dramatists, the Johnny Mercer Writers Colony at Goodspeed Musicals, Florida Repertory Theatre, the Ashland New Play Festival, Orlando Shakespeare Theater, Florida Studio Theatre, the NNPN National New Play Showcase, New Repertory Theatre, the Lark, Actor's Express, the Greenhouse Theatre Center, the Samuel French OOB Short Play Festival, the American Southwest Theatre Company at NMSU, Abbey Theatre in Orlando, and Capital Rep. She was a playwright in residence at Curious, a dramatist guild fellow, and the recipient of a Downstage Left Playwriting Residency at Stage Left Theatre. She was a visiting assistant professor of drama at Kenyon College during the 2011–2012 academic year and taught screenwriting to undergraduates while completing her graduate work at Northwestern University. She has also taught playwrighting to talented high school and middle school dramatists at Interlochen Center for the Arts and Curious Theatre Company and currently writes for television. Here, she talks about a number of key points for all playwrights and students to consider with wise insight.

Q: Could you talk a bit about how you decided to become a playwright? What experiences or influences started you on this journey?

A: Like many playwrights, I am a failed actor. I could never really be in the moment as an actor—I was always outside of it, analyzing what I was saying. I took my first playwrighting class my sophomore year of college, and something just clicked for me. Oddly enough, I found when I was crafting dialogue I could *be* in the moment in a way that felt spontaneous and organic.

Q: How do you, as a writer, determine whether a topic you are interested in writing about is appropriate for the theater as a medium, as opposed to, say, prose or film? Or do you believe that any topic feels right in play format?

A: I went to graduate school for playwrighting, television writing, and screenwriting, so whenever I have a new idea for a story I first ask myself where it belongs. Is this a TV show? Is this a play? Is this a film? You want the story to *demand* that particular medium. I do think it's possible for the same story to exist in more than one medium, but it involves fundamentally changing how the story is told—rethinking the scope, style, and point of view.

Q: How have you approached the task of crafting dialogue most effectively?

A: I always talk out loud as I write—it's important for me to try on the words. See how they feel. See how they fit. It also helps me find all the little idiosyncrasies and repetitions that mimic the way we talk in real life.

Q: What considerations/differences does a playwright need to address when writing original work vs. an adaptation?

A: I think finding your personal connection to the material when adapting is really important, whereas that is usually inherent in original writing. Figuring out why the source material speaks to me, and how I want to speak to it, is always my first step.

Q: What has been your most rewarding experience thus far as a playwright?

A: It's a moment that I've been lucky enough to experience over and over again in my career.

When I gather around a table with a group of artists and dig into a play I've just written. All the questions that come up, all the discussions that get sparked, and all the subsequent changes and revisions that happen after . . . that is, for me, the most rewarding aspect of being a playwright. While I love seeing my work performed in front of an audience, the beginning of the process is always where I feel the most creative and invigorated. It's the moment where I get to hand my blueprint over and see what we can all build together.

SELECTED READINGS

Man of Mystery: William Shakespeare

No doubt you're aware that William Shakespeare, a.k.a. "the Bard of Avon," is pretty much universally considered the greatest theatrical wordsmith of all time. His plays include *Romeo and Juliet*, *Henry V*, *Titus Andronicus*, *The Comedy of Errors*, *A Midsummer Night's Dream*, *Hamlet*, *The Taming of the Shrew*, *The Two Gentlemen of Verona*, *The Merchant of Venice*, *Julius Caesar*, *Much Ado about Nothing*, *Troilus and Cressida*, *All's Well That Ends Well*, *Othello*, *King Lear*, *Antony and Cleopatra*, *Coriolanus*, *The Tempest*, *Cymbeline*, and *The Winter's Tale*; you may have read one or more of them already. What you may not know, however, is that Shakespeare's life was quite colorful and somewhat mysterious. Here are Shakespeare's essential life facts, with a good amount of well-known legend tossed in for good measure:

- He was born on April 23 in Stratford-upon-Avon, UK—maybe. The listed date of April 23 was actually the date he died in 1616—it was thought he was born on the same date but never completely documented.
- He had a large family—seven sisters and brothers—and he married Anne Hathaway while still a teenager. They had three children: Susanna, and twins Hamnet and Judith.
- Shakespeare had a period of "lost" time encompassing several years where no one could ever trace his whereabouts or activities. Rumor had it he was a schoolteacher or horseman during this time—or was he on the run from the authorities for stealing deer? No one ever knew for sure.
- Shakespeare wore an earring—this was considered very daring at the time, and he never explained why he did it.

- To kick off his career, he started his own theater company, the Lord Chamberlain's Men, in London, later known as the King's Men when it was patronized by royalty. His early work was produced by the company and earned wild acclaim. Audiences flocked to the company's productions, making Shakespeare, a wily businessman, independently wealthy. He bought land and real estate and continued to build his riches through his published works.

- Shakespeare's initial published collection of work was called the First Folio. In addition to plays, he wrote sonnets and poems.

- Shakespeare was a gifted actor who often originated his own written characters.

- He utilized a rhythmic, lilting form of speech known as iambic pentameter and wrote his plays in this stylized form. Iambic pentameter contains ten syllables per line, spoken with emphasis on each second syllable, and is taught to actors to this day as a requirement of performing the Bard's works.

- The UK's illustrious Globe Theatre was built by Shakespeare's troupe.

- He drew up his will in March 1616—and died without explanation the following month. No one he knew was aware he was ill, and no explanation for his death has ever been definitively determined. He also disinherited his wife Anne, except for giving her one piece of furniture—a bed. Again, no one ever found out the reason why—and Anne never spoke of any of the circumstances related to his demise. Just another example of Shakespeare's remarkable life and lore.

Rebel With the (Right) Cause: Edward Albee

Edward Albee was, arguably, the father of theatrical reality. The Pulitzer Prize winner took modern playwrighting to its ultimate honesty and wrote about human interaction in a wise, relatable way that will continue to influence playmakers permanently. Yet his work was far from harsh: Albee's message and themes were empathetic and spoke to the heartfelt need all people have to connect to each other. His masterworks included *The Zoo Story*, *The Sandbox*, *Seascape*, *Who's Afraid of Virginia Woolf?*, *Malcolm*, *A Delicate Balance*, *Three Tall Women*, and *The Goat, or Who Is Sylvia?*

Edward Franklin Albee was born on March 12, 1928, and adopted as a baby by his parents Reed and Francis. His father was a theater owner, which was of great interest to Albee as he grew intrigued by the mechanics and emotions of play texts. Albee and his father didn't see eye to eye on much else, though—a restless, troubled young man, Albee displeased his parents immensely by getting expelled from two schools growing up. He attended a military academy, which failed to teach him much discipline, either. Albee managed to graduate from Choate Rosemary Hall in Connecticut and got into Trinity College, but Trinity ended up tossing him out as well.

Albee quickly headed for Greenwich Village, attracted by the freedom and possibility of pursuing a writing career in New York City. He started with *The Zoo Story*, and it was so well received that it quickly got staged in Germany, then moved to Off-Broadway. Albee quickly earned a reputation as one of the most fiercely intelligent, vibrant wits in the theater, and his subsequent play *Who's Afraid of Virginia Woolf?* was considered a game changer on Broadway, with its incredibly frank language and brutal depiction of marital strife. The play earned Albee the first of two Tonys, and he went on to win three Pulitzers, the National Medal of the Arts, and Kennedy Center Honors, to name just a few accolades.

Although he had not been a committed student in his early life, Albee grew to love academia, and enjoyed working with aspiring theater students tremendously throughout his career. He taught at Brandeis University, Johns Hopkins University, and the University of Houston, directing students onstage as well. Albee also established the Edward F. Albee Foundation, a residence and sanctuary for writers and visual artists to develop their work. Albee and his longtime partner, Jonathan Thomas, lived contentedly in Montauk on Long Island, New York, where he passed away on September 16, 2016. His brave work continues to be read and produced all over the world and will no doubt influence generations of playmakers to come.

The Trailblazer: Lorraine Hansberry

Lorraine Hansberry's courage and fierce commitment to authentic self-expression was a hallmark of her fine work as a playwright, as well as her life as a whole. Hansberry became the first African American woman to have her work produced on Broadway when her play *A Raisin in the Sun* debuted in 1959. Her writing was bold and touching, and her commitment to fight for equality is still inspirational decades later.

Hansberry was born on May 19, 1930, and raised in Chicago. Her family legally challenged segregation in their community, a case that went all the way to the Supreme Court, so the young Lorraine grew up determined to fight injustice in every way she could. Hansberry was also academic from an early age; she attended the University of Wisconsin–Madison, the University of Guadalajara in Mexico, and the New School in New York City before taking a job at the political newspaper *Freedom*, where she began writing about politically significant events of the day, specifically black liberation. Hansberry also immersed herself in activist causes, championing civil rights, gay rights, and the antinuclear movement long before it became socially acceptable or fashionable to do so.

Hansberry was also drawn to theater, and began writing in the genre. *A Raisin in the Sun*, her masterwork, explored the difficult lives of black people living in segregation and drew expansively from her own childhood experiences. The play made a huge cultural and creative impact; Hansberry won the New York Critics Circle Award at just twenty-nine, becoming only the fifth woman, first black playwright, and youngest playwright to take this prestigious honor. Audiences flocked to the play, which quickly earned status as a classic. Her next play, *The Sign in Sidney Brustein's Window*, also made an impression on the Great White Way. Unfortunately, Hansberry's life was cut short quickly after she burst into public consciousness; she died of pancreatic cancer at just thirty-four years old in January 1965.

Her work lives on, however. Hansberry's husband, Robert Nemiroff, dedicated himself to ensuring the works she hadn't completed before passing away saw the light of day. Nemiroff personally finished her play *Les Blancs*, adapting many of Hansberry's additional writings into that work. *To Be Young, Gifted and Black*, a play based on Hansberry's life and times, ran from 1968 to 1969 Off-Broadway, and Hansberry inspired the well-known song of the same name by Nina Simone. Then, in 1973, *A Raisin in the Sun* was adapted into the crowd-pleasing musical *Raisin*, which won the 1973 Best Musical Tony award. Decades later, Hansberry's work was introduced to a new audience via the acclaimed 2004 revival of *A Raisin in the Sun* on Broadway, directed by Kenny Leon and starring Sean Combs, Audra McDonald, and Phylicia Rashad (in 2008, the production was also shown on television).

Hansberry's talent has been honored with the establishment of the Lorraine Hansberry Theatre in San Francisco as well as her induction into the American Theater Hall of Fame in 2013. And her most enduring legacy? The courage and conviction of her words on the page, which will continue to evoke thought and inspire change for years to come.

WORKSHEET ASSIGNMENT

Write a character analysis of one of Shakespeare's characters. Focus less on the style of speech the character uses and more on what you can glean about what he or she is saying. What is Juliet's goal? (The freedom to love, as we know.) How does she emotionally set about to attain this? How does she see the obstacles in her way—as surmountable or not? Discern as much as you can about her wants and needs as her character arc moves toward its conclusion.

─────────── **CHAPTER 6 CHECKLIST**───────────

Get more out of what you've learned in this chapter by:

☐ Reading the play *Amadeus* by Peter Shaffer, then watching
Shaffer's adaptation of his work to the 1984 film version,
directed by Miloš Forman. On the page, Shaffer's play is
moving, shocking, sad, and extremely clear in its overall
premise. The excellent 1984 movie *Amadeus* won the Best
Picture Oscar, which was well deserved indeed. Amazingly
honest and bold performances by F. Murray Abraham and
Tom Hulce make the film totally compelling from start to
finish, too. As we discussed earlier, *Amadeus* is a perfect
example of a theme clearly illustrated—Salieri's homicidal
jealousy of Mozart's talent speaks to the larger point that
competition, when taken too far, is a literal poison in life.
By both reading and then viewing the story in its cinematic
context, you'll see how this theme builds toward the story's
climax and understand how a cautionary tale is expertly
constructed for maximum impact.

☐ Writing a dialogue-driven miniscene. Grab your laptop
or a pen and pad and head for the nearest Starbucks.
Look around and choose a pair of people enjoying lattes
and conversation nearby; eavesdrop covertly (it's OK
as long as you don't act weird about it). Listen to what
they're discussing, and jot down the basic points of their
conversation. Zoom in on the most interesting topic they're
talking about—say there's a young guy whose car just broke
down, and he's telling his girlfriend he doesn't have the
cash to get it repaired and is trying to figure out what to
do. Pay attention to how they both express themselves—do
they use a lot of slang? Drop a few "ums" and "uhs"? Note

their cadences. Now, focusing just on that one interesting premise—he wants to find a way to pay for his car to be fixed—write your own version of his dialogue. Add an interesting motivational twist—what if he persuaded his girlfriend to lend him the money? What would her stake in this premise be—would she give him the cash he wants because she likes him or refuse him because she doesn't want him using her? The point of this exercise is not to literally copy their conversation; it's to take the essential situation you're witnessing and lay it out in a creative retelling. Make the two characters say and resolve the issue any way you want to. You'll end up with a short, very realistic take on a situation that's easy to relate to, has an underlying issue to be solved, and thematically details the important topic of manipulation. Finally, ask two student actor friends to read your scene aloud for you once you're finished—you'll be able to evaluate, in real time, whether your writing is clear and your dialogue rings true. A very unique learning opportunity!

7

All about Producing

What does a producer do, anyway? It's a question that sparks more than a little confusion and debate, and that's perfectly understandable. This is because a producer's job is so complicated and intertwined with virtually every element of a theatrical production that the precise scope of his or her duties can seem a little unclear to the layperson.

Simply put, a producer is the supervisor of a show, from top to bottom. This means the producer oversees a show's finances (finding backers to contribute to the show's production costs, plus budgeting the show, and approving all needed expenses), hiring all of the personnel (from the director to the playwright to the designers to approving casting choices), procuring a venue (some producers own their own theater spaces—read more about the Shubert Organization later), working with unions as needed, handling insurance, and negotiating with outside vendors for any supplies or contractual arrangements required to put the production up.

Whew! That's all? Not quite—the producer also oversees the ticketing and publicity campaigns for the production, sets production deadlines with the show's creative team, attends rehearsals to make sure everything is coming together well, and, when it isn't, puts out fires, mediates disputes, and solves any other problem that appears unsolvable.

Thanks to all of that hard work, being a producer can be a pretty profitable enterprise. A producer is usually in line for at least 50 percent of the net profits of a show's total box office and merchandising where applicable. (This depends upon the specific financial arrangement a producer works out with the financial backers of a show.) Although there's an old adage in show business that decrees you should never sink your own cash into a production, many producers do just that and, for their risk, can be rewarded even more handsomely if a show turns a nice profit. Or, on the flip side, a producer could lose every penny put in—which, of course, is great motivation for the producer to make the show as entertaining and crowd pleasing as possible.

Does every show require a producer to be on board? I would argue yes—even a small community show or educational production can benefit from a clearheaded, logical ship captain who thinks several steps ahead during every part of the process. Of course, these kinds of entities don't make a producer lots of money in most cases, but they can provide valuable artistic experiences: the satisfaction of bringing a quality show to the attention of audiences and critics, of shepherding that show to success, gives many budding producers both career experience and earns them well-deserved accolades.

THREE KEY DECISIONS

There are three major decisions a producer invariably needs to get right on a show, no matter how high or low its budget or whether its genre is a straight play or a musical. He or she can do so by asking the following questions:

What Material Is Right to Produce?

Producers read like crazy in order to target exciting new playwrights with fresh work to debut. Producers also comb through existing plays—from classics to underappreciated gems—in order to find the play that will work for his or her creative and financial needs. When evaluating a play, a producer will look at its overall theme (Is it universal? Or is it original enough to cause a stir, therefore interesting large numbers of patrons?). The producer will also look at a play's cast size (shows with smaller casts obviously cost less to produce). Then, he or she will consider the demands of its set and costume needs to make sure they are practical and cost effective to execute.

Who Is the Best Person to Direct This Play?

A producer's choice of director is absolutely paramount to a show's ultimate success or failure. A producer wants to find a director who's smart, imaginative, and has a strong point of view in order to make the play work conceptually. The producer will also want to make sure that the director he or she chooses will be practical; fair and kind to the designers, cast, and crew; and a competent collaborator to discuss all aspects of the production with. A producer will avoid diva directors at all costs if possible—that goes without saying.

How Can I Best Win Attention for This Play?

Theater producers are often stereotyped as flamboyant, colorful salespeople—and yes, in reality, some are very extroverted in this way. Some producers play things closer to the vest, however, and act much more businesslike when drumming up attention for a show with, say, potential investors—which is not to say that a low-key producer isn't equally great at selling. No matter how obvious he or she is about it, a good producer reads his audience (backers, or in a more general sense, an audience demographic, when planning an advertising campaign) and gives the people what they want. The producer could sell the show on the strength of a terrific actor in the lead role, a thrilling plot twist, great musical numbers, or incredible SFX. Being able to identify the sales point or points that will appeal most is the producer's greatest challenge—and the number one requirement for his or her job.

PREPARATION FOR THE JOB

What educational and professional experience should a budding producer pursue? Obviously, a theater arts degree can be a great resource. However, a business background can be even more helpful for many. Study and experience in finance, law, or business administration is strongly advised. It's also incredibly important for a producer to prepare him- or herself by reading and seeing as many plays as possible. Take in good ones, yes, but also the worst shows you can find! There's no better way to learn what truly makes a quality play than comparing the difference with shows that don't work and don't gain any audience foothold.

So which producers throughout theatrical history do the job best? Read on to learn about three legendary pros who got the job really, really right—and earned tremendous respect every step of the way.

SELECTED READINGS

The Savvy Showman: David Merrick

David Merrick not only knew how to garner attention for a play—he also knew how to keep that attention going. The producer of many Broadway hits, including the classic *42nd Street*, Merrick trained and practiced as an attorney; underneath his bigger-than-life persona beat the heart of a highly objective and canny procedural mind.

Merrick, whose real name was David Margulois, was born in St. Louis; he studied at Washington University and St. Louis University School of Law. After toiling as a lawyer for a number of years, he changed his name to the more commercial "Merrick" and decided to break into the theatrical field in 1940. He quickly made his name as a producer who never met a stunt he didn't love. Once, when one of his plays was about to close on Broadway due to weak ticket sales, Merrick found seven men who were New York City residents and happened to share the names of the most influential critics in the city, including the well-respected scribe Walter Kerr. He asked these gentlemen to see his musical *Subways Are for Sleeping*, which had been widely panned. When the men commented positively about the production, Merrick used their words and photos in a newspaper ad. This was the talk of New York, but it sold tickets and bought the production months of extra running time.

Despite his commercial showmanship, Merrick had a commitment to encouraging quality theater in many different ways. His productions were frequently recognized with Tony nominations. His work is highly regarded by many respected theater college programs—for example, he had a theater named in his honor at Brandeis University. Merrick passed away in 1983, but his legacy lives on in the work done by the David Merrick Arts Foundation, which financially and creatively encourages the discovery and development of new musicals that will enrich the American theater for years to come.

The Family Way: Lee, Sam, and Jacob Shubert

Three hardworking brothers with an eye for business and a love of drama made theater history in the early 1900s—and that history continues to pay off today. Lee, Sam, and Jacob Shubert formed the foundation of what is now known as the Shubert Organization, a powerhouse production entity that has owned profitable Broadway theaters for nearly a century.

The Shubert brothers were born in Lithuania and immigrated with their parents and four other siblings to Syracuse, New York, in the 1880s. They became captivated by theater after arriving and, even though they didn't have a lot of work experience, started producing successful local shows. In 1900, the brothers moved to New York City, continuing to produce profitable plays in various spaces. Sam Shubert passed away in 1905, but his siblings carried on, setting their sights on using their show profits to start buying theaters. Financing came easily once the Shuberts' vaudeville company started turning a nationwide profit—they had performances playing steadily in cities like Boston, Philadelphia, and Chicago. They established the Affiliated Theatres Corporation and eventually owned, managed, or rented half of the Broadway theaters in existence and ran fifteen more nationwide. Their incredible success continued; they booked or directly produced over 1,600 shows over the course of their careers until their respective passings (Lee in 1953 and Jacob in 1963).

Today, the brothers' legacy remains incredibly strong. The Shubert Organization has acquired the Winter Garden and Imperial Theatres on Broadway, the National Theatre in Washington, DC, the Shubert Theatre in Boston, and the Sam Shubert Theatre in New York City (since sold to the rival Nederlander Organization producing entity). The company also sold its massive New York City headquarters for close to $300 million in a blockbuster 2016 deal—talk about self-made success.

The Fearless Leader: Joseph Papp

Joe Papp was committed to the idea of creative democracy and boldly decided that Shakespeare's works should not be a privilege enjoyed by the culturally elite only. His dream was to bring these great plays to the masses, and he forged ahead to found the New York Shakespeare Festival, which has brought free theater to New Yorkers in Central Park for decades. He also founded the Off-Broadway Public Theater in Greenwich Village, a space committed to giving new artists a high-profile forum. The plays he produced and championed include *A Chorus Line*.

Born Joseph Papirofsky, and a native of Brooklyn, Papp studied playwrighting as a teenager. His love of the Bard's written word prompted him to start staging free Shakespeare pieces as far back as 1956, on the edge of the East River. Word of mouth spread, the audiences packed each show, and Papp's knack for tireless promotion earned his shows a transfer to Central Park in 1957. To this day, Papp's festival stages two shows each summer at the Delacorte Theater in the park, to the delight of thousands of theater fans who can still watch Shakespeare for nothing.

Papp capitalized on the festivals' success and next sought out an indoor space to produce new work. He rented the Astor Library building from the city of New York, right before it was scheduled to be demolished, and named it the Joseph Papp Public Theater. The Public showcased the early work of some of the most exciting new writers in the theater, including David Rabe. Papp produced modern classics such as *Hair, for colored girls who have considered suicide / when the rainbow is enuf,* and *The Normal Heart,* and he backed *A Chorus Line* from its initial workshop stage to its Broadway triumph, due to his deep belief in and respect for its creator, Michael Bennett.

Papp supported the development of a number of Off-Broadway theaters, including the Riverside Shakespeare Company, and also spearheaded a campaign to preserve older theater houses throughout Manhattan.

He passed away in 1991 after battling prostate cancer, but his vibrant philosophy of theatrical discovery continues to live on at the Public, with every new playwright whose work earns a place there.

────────── CHAPTER 7 CHECKLIST ──────────

Get more out of what you've learned in this chapter by:

☐ Reading *Great Producers: Visionaries of the American Theater* by Iris Dorbian (Allworth Press). A riveting, detailed examination of the lives and success of top producers throughout the decades, from Flo Ziegfeld to Fran and Barry Weissler and every significant professional in between.

☐ Watching producer David Binder's fascinating TED talk (www.ted.com/playlists/393/talks_for_theater-geeks). Binder discusses how his experience at an arts festival in Australia opened him up to the importance of individual cities distinguishing themselves in an individual theatrical sense. A great discussion on the importance of grassroots production.

8

All about Designing

A single, powerful spotlight. A dusty, haunted mansion. Booming thunder. A breathtaking mountainous backdrop where no hills could really exist. A gorgeous silk corseted gown. Each of these indelible, illuminating stage images is the work of a lighting, scenic, sound, projection, and costume designer—just imagine what our contemporary, sensory theatrical experience would be like without their amazing efforts.

Design is an incredibly important aspect of a production's effectiveness. A designer's job is to illustrate the themes and story of a play, while at the same time helping the play's director convey a very specific vision and viewpoint in interpreting this material. Designers must be artistically fluent, as well as technically proficient, in order to accomplish these crucial tasks. Being a designer requires a huge amount of dedication, insight, long hours, and faultless attention to detail.

This chapter covers the fundamental components of stage design, from its initial conception to its technical execution in a production.

Let's talk about specific types of designers and what their work consists of.

LIGHTING DESIGN

Lighting designers create a great element of ambience, atmosphere, and environment for a play. Think about the intense vibe lighting may have created in the plays you've personally seen: a dark night, a brilliantly sunny scene, or a colorful kaleidoscope in an experimental scene can truly enhance the scene's message and impact.

Lighting designers work very closely with the director of a play to choose, early on, what their lighting needs to do to complement the director's intention, scene by scene, for a production. A lighting designer reads a play a number of times so he or she understands the settings and subtexts of all the points in the text. Next, the lighting designer creates a lighting plot from photos, storyboards, computer software, and the input of the production's scenic and costume designers so the "look" of the play will communicate a cohesive statement.

When the lighting plot is complete, the designer implements it within the theater, hanging lights, using colored lighting gels and dimmers, programming computerized effects into the lighting board, and supervising the lighting crew's execution of the lighting cues within the show.

SCENIC/SET DESIGN

A show's scenic designer establishes a strong visual "story" in creating and/or sourcing set pieces for a production. Again, the scenic designer works very closely with the director in order to get every portion of the show's set looking as accurate in regard to the director's overall vision as possible.

After studying the script inside out, a show's scenic designer will typically sketch out ideas for how the set will look and will additionally draw up floor plans of the stage and often a model of the set as well.

Budgeting, contacting suppliers, purchasing supplies, and building/painting the set with a set run crew are the next duties at hand. A set designer will also keep abreast of blocking during rehearsals, to determine how set pieces may need to be adjusted, and will work out any set changes that may be necessary during the show's run.

COSTUME DESIGN

A show's costume designer helps the director and actors descriptively show many aspects of a character's personality and traits through the clothing that character wears onstage. The costume designer also helps visually establish the show's era and societal environment and may often design garments that symbolically move the play's story line forward.

The costume designer studies the play's script, then makes elaborate sketches detailing every visual aspect of each character's garments.

He or she also consults with the show's other designers to coordinate colors and make certain fabric choices that will look appropriate in conjunction with the lighting and scenic details. Once the director approves the costume sketches, the designer will purchase fabric and supplies through a strict budget, cut patterns, and, with a crew, sew, or "build," each costume. The costume designer schedules fittings with each actor and coordinates any "quick changes" that will take place during the show's run. He or she also rounds up and organizes the jewelry, hats, gloves, and other accessories each costume requires as a finishing touch. If actors are wearing wigs, often the costume designer will be responsible for selecting and styling those as well.

SOUND DESIGN

A sound designer is responsible for creating, choosing, and executing all the atmospheric noises necessary within a play. This may mean the sound designer records natural sounds, like birds singing, or searches computer programs or the web for prerecorded effects. The sound designer of a show carefully goes through its script to find any sounds mentioned in the text and works with the director on additional sound effects that will be worked into the production. Additionally, any prerecorded music cues or voice-overs are the sound designer's job to execute.

Sound designers can also employ more DIY elements like a "crash-box," or sound effects tool (more on that in a bit), or coordinating shouts and handclaps, for example, from cast and crew backstage. The sound designer writes all the sound cues he or she is using into the script and supervises the show's sound operator or the crew member who runs the sound effects board and plays the effects during the show.

PROJECTION DESIGN

A projection designer uses computerized images to build a background viewscape in a production. Projections may take the place of actual scenic backdrops or painted flats or may be used in conjunction with them. Words, numbers, character photographs—any of these details can be projected onstage as part of a production's thematic message and visual statement.

For any given production, a projection designer will choose moving or still images from stock video or photo sources or will photograph or design original images to be projected, often in close collaboration with the set designer. The completed images are edited and loaded into a piece of equipment called a media server, a computerized device that stores images and actually projects them onto the stage. Projectors may also be hung around the stage or house by the projection designer, depending upon the angle of a desired effect. The lighting designer of a show is always the projection designer's best buddy; together, they strive to coordinate the visual look of the show and make sure neither projections nor lighting effects clash with, or overwhelm, each other.

This is the main point of design as a whole. It's a balancing act; designers work together to complement, not compete, in every production they tackle. Design is democratic, it's unifying, it's universally descriptive, and it's the color we most often remember after we leave an affecting performance.

———————— **SELECTED READING** ————————

Big Bang Boom

Adrian Bridges is a New York City–based guitarist, composer, actor, and sound designer who employs historical perspective, strong technique, and collaboration in every facet of his work. What Bridges does so uniquely is approach the task of sound design for the theater from a distinctly original musical perspective. An intriguing example of how he blended his musical and production sound expertise was the play *Solstice Party*, held at the ART/New York Theatres and for which he wrote, directed, and scored original music that complemented the show's soundscape.

Here, Bridges discusses how he melds his creative musical influences with his technical work so seamlessly.

Q: Could you speak a bit about what sparked your interest in theater? What made you want to pursue the diverse creative/technical paths of both acting and sound design?

A: I first got the music bug when I was four years old, after encountering the Beatles. I immersed myself in their music and their contemporaries' music as a kid and began studying classical guitar formally when I was six. By age ten, I knew I wanted to pursue a career in music. I first discovered the magic of theater in my tenth-grade English class, where I had an amazing teacher who got us both writing and acting original and excerpted classics, including Edward Albee and Tennessee Williams, alongside Shakespeare and Sophocles. I was really set on becoming a musician though, so while I earned a National Young Playwrights runner-up through her class, I never seriously thought that was a path I'd pursue.

I first realized theater could be a part of my career as a sophomore in college at New York University, where I played in the pit orchestra for a mainstage production of Jeanine Tesori's *Violet*. In that show, I got to alternate between two guitars, banjo, and mandolin, in all of my favorite musical styles, ranging from gospel and blues to bluegrass and rock 'n' roll. I'd never seen such authentic use of American music in a theatrical piece, and I went on to play in a lot of pit orchestras in college. Pit orchestras are really hidden away, though, and I love performing for an audience, so when friends in theater circles offered me opportunities to play music as a character onstage, I jumped at the chance. Those roles have been the most fulfilling for me, where I get to both work on the production and performance ends of a piece.

As a musician, I've always balanced my ambitions as a composer and performer across many different genres, so theater has only broadened the scope of my artistic ambitions. The creative and design team has the most influence on the shape of a piece, and few things are as enjoyable as bringing new art to life, but nothing is as exhilarating as performing. Composing and developing a piece is like a slow burn compared to the quick burst of energy that comes as a performer, so having both in balance is something I relish.

I was first asked to do sound design by an elementary school peer while I was in college, and I quickly came to realize that it opened up a whole new palette for me to play with as a composer. I find now that I often use sound elements in my music and musical colors in my sound design. You can hear plenty of sound design on my hip-hop group's album, and I believe approaching sound as a musician, pulling out textures like an orchestra conductor, has given a certain humanity to my work that people seem to respond to. Often, when I see shows, I find sound follows the technical needs of the piece, dropped in here and there around the dialogue, as opposed to pushing the action in the way that our natural environments do to us every day.

Q: What is a day in your life like as a sound designer? Could you talk a bit to readers in overview form about how you choose audio

elements for a production, then incorporate them into a show so they work seamlessly?

A: Typically, a director or producer will send me a script with some very broad notes. I'll read the script and mark every moment I think could be elevated by some form of sound design. Then I'll send along my sound outline of the piece and talk through it with the director to see how our visions can come together. Most of my work as a sound designer happens before we walk into a tech rehearsal, and speakers are portable in a way that light grids are not, so I try to develop as many of the crucial moments as quickly as possible both to get feedback from the director and to try things out in rehearsal. I love being in the room when a piece is coming together. Traditionally that space is reserved for actors and directors, but by waiting till tech rehearsal, design contributions rarely end up as more than window dressing. I try to find ways that sound can integrate into those early choices, so the actors can rely on it as another element they can bounce their performance off and the director can build blocking around my choices as opposed to vice versa.

Developing the sonic atmosphere of a piece involves me going through that outline I've made and scouring my personal sound archives and the Internet for textures that evoke the mood I'm looking for. Depending on how big a scale the production is, there are often sounds I'll record myself as well, either at home or in a specific location. Then I may modify the audio I capture in Pro Tools (an audio editing software) so it sounds distant or close, cosmic or flat; and I'll layer several different clips of sound together for the show. If I'm creating a beach, I'll add rich crashing waves as well as light, frothy ones, a whipping wind, and perhaps some seagulls. A forest may include light wind blowing through the leaves (or just branches if it's winter), bugs of different varieties matched to the climate or time of day, and birds chirping. With these different layers I can create an immersive landscape, putting different elements louder or softer in different speakers, and I can modulate the balance when we get in the room for theater. And in case the director has different ideas in rehearsal, I make sure to bring a couple different types of each sound to give them options.

Q: What do you love most about working in the theater?

A: I love the moment when you try out something new in rehearsal or performance that lands just perfectly. Theater is a multidisciplinary collaborative art form, so when all the design elements or acting performances line up and come together, it's magical to see it all sync up. In music, we talk about sympathetic vibrations, which allow notes to resonate louder when they share the same overtones. A chord is stronger than a note, and a mixed-media piece of art is greater than the sum of its parts.

————— WORKSHEET ASSIGNMENT—————

Google a photo of a scene from the play of your choice—a Broadway show, a regional production, or a student production. No matter what play you select, it should be a play you have already seen or read. Write an analysis of how you think the visual elements of the play help tell the story and advance/enhance the scene's action.

———————— CHAPTER 8 CHECKLIST ————————

Get more out of what you've learned in this chapter by:

- ☐ Making a crashbox. This nifty sound design tool can create big, smashing sound effects with minimal effort but a lot of your personal creativity. Grab a thick cardboard box, and fill it with noisy debris—broken dishes, old tin cans, old holiday bells, stray silverware. Experiment with different discarded items by putting things in, shaking the box, then taking out what doesn't sound loud enough or doesn't work for your taste. When you're happy with how your box sounds, tape up all openings with duct tape (two layers for security), then drop it to your heart's content! Excellent for a variety of effects in any given show.

- ☐ Trying your hand at costume sketches. Draw a croquis, which is the basic image of a human figure, or model, that a costume designer illustrates his or her designs on. It's easy: scour the web, fashion magazines, or books for a photo of a simply dressed man or woman performing a simple physical gesture—walking, or just posing with arms at their sides. Trace the image on paper, make multiple copies, and then use it as a template to draw costume ideas over. Practicing extensively on a croquis is how many costume designers learn how their creations visually move and flow, so draw as much as you can!

- ☐ Getting inspired by a great designer. Choosing an accomplished role model is a great idea for aspiring theater designers. Find an amazing, superachieving professional designer to learn about online, and make it your business to study their work by seeing live performances they've worked on in person or on YouTube. Here are some wonderful artists to consider:

Wendall K. Harrington

Known as the "godmother of theater projection," Harrington's projection designs have graced esteemed Broadway productions like *The Who's Tommy*, *The Elephant Man*, *Grey Gardens*, and *Beauty and the Beast*; she's also a professor at the Yale School of Drama.

Abe Jacobs

A legendary Broadway sound designer who got his start working with rock and roll superstar Jimi Hendrix. Jacobs has designed scores of epic shows, from *Cats* to *Evita* to *Joseph and the Amazing Technicolor Dreamcoat*.

Jennifer Tipton

An incredibly creative lighting designer whose beautiful and evocative designs have been pivotal to many regional and Broadway productions, including *Our Town*, *The Cherry Orchard*, and *Jerome Robbins' Broadway*.

Santo Loquasto

A visionary, incredibly diverse scenic and costume designer whose genius is exemplified in classic Broadway productions of *Grand Hotel*, *Glengarry Glen Ross*, *Waiting for Godot*, and *Hello, Dolly!*

Tony Walton

A scenic and costume design icon, Walton's highly influential Broadway work has spanned the gamut from *A Funny Thing Happened on the Way to the Forum* to *Pippin* to *Chicago* to *Uncle Vanya*.

9

All about Musical Theater

A stage musical can take many forms indeed. If you haven't seen more than a musical theater production or two, you might be under the impression that this genre is very traditional—and yes, maybe a little corny, given that people may seem to randomly burst into song out of nowhere at any given moment in a show's plot. Yet musical theater is one of the most logical, diverse, smart, and intriguing artistic experiences you can take in. You can enjoy a classic musical comedy like *Guys and Dolls*; a daring political rock musical like *Hair*; or a melodic, socially relevant statement on the challenges today's young people face like *Dear Evan Hansen*. The more musicals you watch, the more you'll start to innately understand the structure and intention of their construction, which supports the themes that a musical communicates.

In this chapter, we'll examine the musical in a way that cracks open its importance and history; you'll quickly notice that the genre is extremely flexible in terms of the way it can be written and performed, leading to great opportunities for artistic expression. We'll learn about the origins and through line of the musical's journey and discover the brilliance of some of its most vital contributors throughout the years. And we'll discuss the strong emotional elements musical theater conveys: pure joy, deep sorrow, burning love. A musical's songs are the perfect vessel to deliver feelings that pack the biggest punch you can imagine and touch your heart in ways you probably never expected.

THE DEVELOPMENT OF MUSICAL THEATER AS AN ART FORM

Back in the time of the ancient Greeks and the Romans, music was often utilized in many plays, especially in commedia dell'arte. One could say, then, that musical theater really started at that time. Not quite so fast, though. In the nineteenth century, opera really set the basic template for the form of musical theater we know and appreciate today. Ballad opera, which incorporated familiar songs into its plots, was particularly popular in England. Then comic opera gained popularity, engineered to a great extent by the composer Jacques Offenbach. Offenbach was quite prolific, authoring over 150 pieces that poked fun at politics and historic figures like Napoleon. Composers W. S. Gilbert and Arthur Sullivan then moved comic opera into its next stage, composing audience-pleasing operettas, including *The Pirates of Penzance*, *Ruddigore*, *Iolanthe*, and many more pieces that are still performed today. Gilbert and Sullivan revolutionized the concept of adding serious themes to the musical stage piece, as their work criticized the British government in a way considered bold at the time.

In the US, *The Black Crook*, produced in 1866 at the Niblo's Garden building in New York City, essentially started the format of the stage musical we know today. Its story was written by Charles M. Barras, containing both new songs and adaptations of familiar tunes of the day. This show marked the first time song and dance were integrated into a plot onstage and was a very big hit, later touring and enjoying Broadway revivals. Vaudeville was also very influential in setting the stage for the development of musicals in the US. From the 1880s all the way through to the 1930s, vaudeville shows consisting of several brief musical acts became incredibly popular, leading to the opening of vaudeville theater venues in major cities (with such legendary names as the Pantages and the Orpheum). In 1927, the musical was truly born when Jerome Kern and Oscar Hammerstein crafted *Show Boat*. *Show Boat* was highly original in its use of honest, relatable emotional situations as a catalyst for action and felt very contemporary, not period. Audiences responded with great approval to the clarity of *Show Boat*'s book, the seamless way its songs were woven into its plot, and the aural beauty of its score.

Show Boat also became a clear early example of the "book" musical format that has become standard. The "book" of a musical is its story, including its plot and characters, and its "score" is the collection of songs that propel that story forward. Text and music are interspersed throughout a book musical—usually four to six main songs lay out the important elements of the musical's plot, sequentially from the start of the play. Most book musicals consist of two acts but also can be performed in a shorter one-act structure. Also, a musical revue format is a popular structure—within a musical revue, songs (and sometimes scenes), often from adapted sources, are linked together to tell a story. Songs within a musical are intended to act as a window into the soul of a character, the conduit by which a composer can relate how that character either covertly or overtly feels. This is why musicals often are marked by highly emotional peaks and valleys—their characters' plights, victories, and progression are worn completely on their musical sleeves. (Now, does a it make a little more sense as to why folks start singing with such feeling during the course of a musical? Sure! Now you'll watch one much differently.)

A musical also incorporates dance as an interpretive tool in telling its story. A choreographer will create movements that translate the emotional themes of a given theme or song, be those themes happy, sad, or anywhere in between. The musical arrangements will also reflect the emotions expressed in each song. What kind of musical accompaniment is utilized in any given piece is highly subjective: some shows call for a big orchestra complete with conductor and concertmaster, while others might find the perfect fit with a small ensemble. It all depends on the nature of the musical's material, its writing team's directions, and the show's director's interpretation.

LANDMARK MODERN MUSICALS

The following musicals are widely considered to be the greatest examples of the art form available to see (live or on YouTube), listen to (via their original Broadway cast recordings), or read. Study as many as you can to see how different the specific styles of both book and score writing can be yet how clear and cohesive each musical is in terms of plot and emotional impact.

42nd Street
American Idiot
Annie
The Book of Mormon
Bye Bye Birdie
Cabaret
Cats
Chicago
A Chorus Line
Damn Yankees
Evita
Fiddler on the Roof
Funny Girl
A Funny Thing Happened on the Way to the Forum
Grease
Guys and Dolls
Gypsy
Hamilton
Hello, Dolly!

In the Heights
The King and I
Kiss Me, Kate
Les Misérables
Man of La Mancha
Monty Python's Spamalot
The Music Man
My Fair Lady
The Mystery of Edwin Drood
Nine
Once
The Pajama Game
The Phantom of the Opera
Pippin
The Producers
Rent
The Sound of Music
South Pacific
Spring Awakening
Sunday in the Park with George
Sweeney Todd
West Side Story
Wicked
The Wiz
Wonderful Town

—————————SELECTED READINGS————————

The Intellectual Tunesmith: Richard Rodgers

Richard Rodgers was a composer of unfailing work ethic, grand talent, and fierce intelligence. He composed forty-three Broadway musicals and served as writing partner to both Oscar Hammerstein and Lorenz Hart. Rodgers's work includes the seminal shows *Oklahoma!*, *Carousel*, *South Pacific*, *The King and I*, and *The Sound of Music*. He won a Pulitzer Prize, plus the Emmy, Oscar, Tony, and Grammy Awards.

He was born in Queens, New York; a good student, Rodgers was accepted to prestigious Columbia University. He attended many Broadway shows when he was young, which sparked his interest in the possibility of writing music—so much so that he decided to transfer to what is now the Juilliard School to focus on composition. After college, Rodgers was introduced to his collaborator Hart through a mutual friend; in short order, the two wrote the song "Any Old Place With You," which landed in the Broadway musical *A Lonely Romeo*. They went on to write *Dearest Enemy*, *The Girl Friend*, *Peggy-Ann*, *A Connecticut Yankee*, and *Present Arms*, all which made it to the Great White Way and cemented their reputation as a stellar songwriting team. The duo had further success writing Hollywood musicals before a second golden period on Broadway, when Rodgers and Hart produced songs for *On Your Toes*, *Babes in Arms*, and *The Boys from Syracuse*. Hart's death ended their partnership.

Rodgers rebounded by restarting his work with a previous collaborator, Oscar Hammerstein. The two toiled to create *Oklahoma!*, which was lauded as a masterpiece when it debuted in 1943 due to its innovative melding of song, story, dance, and an engaging plot. After they had worked for over two decades, Hammerstein also passed away; Rodgers went on to excel at solo composition, as well as new and exciting partnerships with Stephen Sondheim and Martin Charnin. Rodgers passed away in 1979; in 1990, the Richard Rodgers Theatre was named in his honor on Broadway at Forty-Sixth Street, where it remains an incredibly popular institution.

The Peerless Voice: Ethel Merman

Ethel Merman's big, brassy, bell-clear mezzo voice was a miracle in itself—a natural gift masterfully and perfectly utilized. Merman's trademark belt lit up Broadway in shows ranging from *Gypsy* to *Anything Goes* to *Annie Get Your Gun*. She became most famous for her rousing rendition of "There's No Business Like Show Business," which she performed for decades on screen and onstage.

Born in 1908 in Queens, New York, Merman loved music from an early age. Her parents took her to watch performers like Sophie Tucker and Fanny Brice, and she taught herself to sing from sheet music. (Incredibly, she never took a single singing lesson.) After high school, while working in the business sector by day, Merman performed at private parties by night, then moved on to nightclub singing. She was discovered by an agent, who got her a film contract; she then was cast in the stage musical *Girl Crazy*, where she originated the popular standard "I Got Rhythm." She went on to make her mark in shows like *Take a Chance*, then performed in five Cole Porter musicals, including her vivacious star turn in *Anything Goes*. She played the title role in *Annie Get Your Gun* for over three years on Broadway, then won a Tony for her masterful performance in *Call Me Madam*.

In 1959, Merman took on her most lauded performance, that of villainous mom Rose in *Gypsy*. Later in her career, she starred in *Hello, Dolly!*; as theater lore has it, her first performance in the 1970 staging was so good that she was constantly interrupted during her songs and dialogue by standing ovations from the audience, an unprecedented honor. Merman subsequently appeared in many TV shows and films (including the classic comedy *Airplane!*), and, known for her big heart, spent her free time volunteering in a New York City Hospital.

She was married four times, including, quite infamously, to actor Ernest Borgnine for just a little over a month. Merman had two children and passed away in 1984 after battling brain cancer.

The Torchbearer: Lin-Manuel Miranda

Lin-Manuel Miranda's many talents are infusing the current theater scene with a new lifeblood; the sky's the limit as far as his future is concerned. The author and star of *Hamilton*, arguably the most popular modern musical of all time, Miranda's intense performance style and free-flowing writing ability is filled with joy and enthusiasm, and those qualities infuse his work in every way.

Born in 1979 in New York City, Miranda spent a lot of time in Puerto Rico with his grandparents as well. His father, a consultant to the Democratic Party, exposed him to politics at a young age; Miranda wrote jingles for candidates' campaigns, including one used in Eliot Spitzer's bid for New York governor when Miranda was only a teenager. His gift for songwriting and love of music spurred him to cofound a hip-hop troupe while attending Wesleyan University. He wrote *In the Heights*, a rap-influenced musical that later became a Broadway classic, while he was just a sophomore, staging its world premiere while he was still in school. After graduation, Miranda brought *In the Heights* Off-Broadway, where it became a smash. The show transferred to Broadway in 2008, and in true Cinderella style, won four Tony Awards, including Best Musical.

Miranda started working on his next show after reading a biography of Alexander Hamilton. He debuted *The Hamilton Mixtape*, a cutting of music for the show, in the presence of President Barack Obama at the White House in 2009; he opened the full version of *Hamilton* at the Public Theater in 2015, after extensive writing and planning. The show quickly transferred to Broadway, breaking box-office records as soon as it opened in August 2015, and it continues to be the theater world's biggest hit in New York, in London, and in regional/touring productions.

Miranda also cowrote the Broadway musical *Bring It On*, appeared on TV shows ranging from *Modern Family* to *Curb Your Enthusiasm* (where he re-created the famed *Hamilton* duel with Larry David), and was nominated for a Best Original Song Oscar for "How Far I'll Go" from the Disney film *Moana*. His future projects include composing songs for a live-action version of *The Little Mermaid*, and he is a tireless advocate and fund-raiser for Puerto Rico's rebuilding efforts following the 2017 hurricane that devastated the island. Married to attorney Vanessa Nadal, Miranda is proud dad to sons Sebastian and Francisco.

———————— CHAPTER 9 CHECKLIST ————————

Get more out of what you've learned in this chapter by:

☐ Watching a film musical. The 2008 movie adaptation of *Mamma Mia!* and its 2018 sequel *Mamma Mia! Here We Go Again* are two fun suggestions to start with. When watching a musical adapted to film, it's very helpful to have seen a stage version of the play as well, either live or on YouTube. This way, you can compare and contrast. For instance, you can easily see the difference regarding the way a musical is expanded out on film—most obviously, in terms of real-world setting and location. It's very interesting to note how the feeling of a musical changes when it's freed from the confines of a limited world onstage (and, in the case of the *Mamma Mia!* films, transplanted to a sunny Greek island). Does this enhance or take away from the source material? Write your own review and express your impressions.

PART TWO
Skill in Motion

10
Getting Technical

Theater is magical, to a great extent—in both a figurative and literal sense. The figurative part: human ingenuity, emotional expression, and imagination. The literal part: technical wizardry and expertise, which allows those mystical, beautiful aspects of creativity to fully flourish. The technicians who make it work, then, are the real magicians behind the curtain.

So how do these talented thespians perform their complicated sleight-of-hand? Through hard work and nitty-gritty knowledge. This chapter focuses on the role of technical work in a theatrical production, in terms of how pieces of stagecraft fit together to bring a production to its fullest, liveliest potential. Let's break down a number of key positions, in terms of responsibilities, function, and importance to every show as a whole.

STAGE MANAGEMENT

A stage manager, or SM, is thought of as the director's right hand by most theater personnel, and that assumption is quite true. An equally accurate way to regard a stage manager, though, is as the workhorse engine that keeps the great big bus of a production on the road without breaking down. A production's stage manager assists the director on all technical matters, coordinates details with the design team, supervises the cast and crew, runs all rehearsals, calls the show's cues during performances, and constantly solves problems, deals with emergencies, and manages personalities.

Basically the stage manager is the ultimate jack- or jill-of-all-trades on a show.

A stage manager's job starts with planning and running auditions for the director; when a cast is chosen, the SM posts this info on a production call board, the central physical source of info at the theater for cast and crew. The SM is responsible for all paperwork associated with a show: contact sheets, a promptbook filled with all of the blocking, cues, notes, schedules, tasks, lists, logs, and script data to be used during rehearsals and performances. Many SMs also prepare a separate "production book," which serves as a record of rehearsals, meetings, and business-related paperwork as well.

In a show's rehearsal space, the SM "spikes," or tape marks, the spots on the floor where set pieces will be, and puts in rehearsal furniture for the actors. The SM takes blocking notes as the director stages the show, and stays on-book to keep everyone's place during rehearsals and to help actors out in the moment if they forget a line. When it's time for dry and wet tech, the stage manager supervises the load-in of the set and hanging of lighting equipment, then sets and calls the lighting, sound, projection and set cues, cementing the way technical effects will play out during performances. The SM runs all technical procedures of the production during its whole run, then supervises strike at the rehearsals, in order to supervise and assist in the technical aspects of the mounting the show.

TECHNICAL DIRECTING

Many productions and/or theaters employ a technical director, or TD. Basically, a TD's duties are operational, in terms of maintaining and using all technical equipment correctly, plus making sure all production procedures are safe for cast and crew. A TD is also heavily involved in planning which technical equipment, like lighting and sound items, that designers and technicians will need for a show and securing that needed equipment.

TDs also set up equipment, work with designers on specific lighting plots and sound requirements, help supervise load-ins and strikes, and make themselves pretty much indispensable when it comes to answering questions about the theater itself or how any technical issue can best be solved. The TD also supervises set construction, orders supplies, works on technical budgets for individual shows and the theater in general, and trains crew members and technical staff on an ongoing basis.

PROPS MASTERY

A props master has jurisdiction over all of the props and some small set pieces in a production. The props master will locate, buy, or pull from theater storage all of the pieces needed for rehearsal (sometimes items in less-than-perfect condition, which will later be replaced by new, higher-quality "production props").

How does the props master know what props will be needed? A couple of different ways. First, obviously, by reading the script carefully, and making notes of all obligatory objects mentioned in the text. Next, by speaking with the director about his or her prop preferences and consulting with the set designer as to small pieces, or "hand props," that might be integral to the show's scenic plot. All of this info goes onto a master prop list that the props master uses for the length of the production.

Props masters usually love the thrill of the hunt. They're very adept at scoring vintage props at the flea market or local Salvation Army, and can suss out unusual items online easily. Props masters are usually on a pretty tight budget, so crafty PMs are also artisans: building props from old materials, or in conjunction with the set designer, can be a creative and economical way to include hard-to-find or elaborate pieces.

MASTER ELECTRICIAN WORK

A master electrician, or ME, helps the lighting designer manifest every technical detail of the lighting plot in a production. The job is similar to being the technical director for the lighting designer. The ME supervises the hanging of lighting equipment, trains the lighting board operator regarding cues for a production, does circuiting and wiring work, and serves as the lighting designer's second set of eyes during technical rehearsals to make sure every effect is being crafted correctly.

An ME also runs "light check" before every show's performances: this is a systematic exercise in which each light is tested individually, and adjustments or repairs are needed to make sure all the equipment is a go.

STAGEHAND WORK

As you probably know, stagehands do a lot of the heavy lifting on a production. They load in set pieces and props; set up lighting and sound equipment; assemble large segments of platforms, rises, and onstage staircases; safety-test equipment; plug in microphones; move flats; help set construction crews complete building jobs—and that's just the start of their week! Stagehands also "run" a show, meaning that they remain in the wings, or in assigned spots throughout the house, to pull the curtain, move set pieces or furniture on- or offstage during set changes, and operate specialized equipment (like flies, winches, and wheeled platforms). Stagehands also keep the stage area clean and organized, perform key labor during strikes, and lend a hand whenever the SM or designers may need a little something extra taken care of.

All in all, stage technicians are cool, calm, and collected miracle workers. They stay very much in the moment, focus on what needs to be done logically, and deliver. This kind of professionalism can serve as a timely and welcome example to more high-strung members of a company—like a nervous actor or temperamental director—at the most heated points in production (like dress rehearsal or opening night). Always respect your techs—they really deserve it.

SELECTED READING

Unsung Heroes: How Theater Techs Save the Day

When it comes to getting glory and praise on any given production, the director and cast are invariably first in line. It makes sense: after all, the director's vision is a show's driving force, as we know, and great actors are the most visible example of the hard work *every* company member puts into a show. Behind the scenes, too, theater insiders know that the producer, playwright, designers, and stage manager contribute incredibly in their leading roles on a production as well.

So who are the unsung heroes of every show? As we've just discussed, the production's hardworking crew members are paramount. The crew is the heart and soul of what makes a production run smoothly and deserve many accolades for that. Yet among those tech workers, there are five key positions that almost never receive any positive, singled-out notice. These are exceptionally difficult jobs! So, in this chapter, we salute these often-overlooked but incredibly crucial folks who really do the dirty work. They sacrifice credit to tackle the unglamorous jobs no one else wants to do: to keep actors and crew safe in dicey situations, to build confidence in a cast member's work as that cast member is building a character, and to accurately depict the tiniest details of a show's look. Their work is vital and important, and very much worth taking on; after learning about what each of these tech jobs requires, do you think you might be interested in giving any of them a whirl?

Job #1: Assistant Stage Manager (ASM)

Few jobs are as time sucking and thankless as that of ASM—but there's no better way to learn the inner workings of a production, either. An ASM, as the title indicates, is basically the assistant to the stage manager but with the added responsibility of supervising the work of the crew members during a show's run. The ASM of a production is expected to be very punctual and to hold everyone else (crew and actors) to that same prompt standard.

Here's a sample list of the ASM's duties:

- Preparing the space before rehearsals—sweeping, taping the floor to indicate location of set pieces, emptying trash, and pulling set pieces and props from stock and setting them up for the actors to use.
- Gathering actors' contact info and chasing after and reprimanding latecomers to rehearsal (or, worst-case scenario, performances).
- Copying, handing out, and storing script copies.
- Helping with blocking notes.
- Staying on-book to help actors who forget their lines and to keep the place for the director as he or she runs scenes.
- Checking daily on progress with costume run issues and set preparation.
- Having a working knowledge of every set run crew position so he or she can jump in to any job in an emergency situation.
- Training all crew members in their varied positions.
- Supervising the stage area during each performance, putting out any imaginable fire while the stage manager is busy calling the show's cues.
- Fixing, on the spot, any mistakes crew members make during rehearsals and performances.
- Helping actors who run into any trouble during a performance or rehearsal, from forgetting an entrance to falling ill unexpectedly.
- Cleaning up after every rehearsal and performance, and locking up the rehearsal/performance space.
- Taking responsibility for any rented or borrowed props, set pieces, or scenery.

Obviously, an ASM needs nerves of steel, a great memory, a knack for organization, and the ability to multitask effectively. At a *minimum*. The great thing about being an ASM, though, is that the work prepares you for virtually any production position you might want to tackle next—from SM to director to a specific crew job you might discover you really love. You can take great pride, and build a strong sense of self-confidence, too, at being able to handle the tough tasks that go with being an ASM.

Job #2: Rigger

A rigging position is hugely important when it comes to safely anchoring, securing, and running equipment during a production. A rigger needs to be highly skilled in terms of understanding how to work with heavy loads, flies, pulleys, cables, and other machinery. He or she must research, prep, run, and strike all of these types of equipment in accordance with strict industry standards as well.

Here's a sample list of a rigger's duties:

- Inspect a theater space and its set at load-in for any safety issues that would preclude using flies, cables, pulleys, or any additional equipment during a production. Put solving any such issues into motion by working with the show's tech director, stage manager, and crew before doing anything else.
- Procure any necessary equipment for the theater or production that isn't already on-site.
- Ensure that all rigging equipment is the proper weight and size for the production venue and the needs of the production.
- Anchor equipment using proper alignment and leveling techniques.
- Attach loads, or weights, to rigged pieces of the set so they don't fall.

- Attach cables or pulleys to equipment so it can be moved or flown.
- Safety-check and install flies, if used in a production.
- Secure set pieces to any flies, or work with actors who will be flown in harnesses if applicable.
- Have advanced skills with all tools, especially complex power tools.
- Safely attach pulleys, blocks, and cables to ceiling poles and beams as needed.
- Calculate the plan for moving heavy set pieces or equipment on- and offstage, and supervise/execute this movement.
- Set up and test all rigging equipment before every show.
- Run rigging equipment during the show, including operating cables, pulleys, flies, winches, and set pieces.
- Make all repairs to rigging or rigged equipment during tech rehearsals and show run.
- Act as a safety spotter during tech rehearsals and show run, and make sure all cast and crew members know how to safely work with and around the rigging equipment.
- Strike, store, and/or return all rigging equipment after the show run.

Rigging isn't a job that you just breeze right into; riggers must train in a technical theater arts program and pass an extensive exam in order to earn their right to do the work. If you're willing to put in the time and hard work, though, it's very rewarding to know your efforts are making set operations run smoothly and that your expertise is keeping the personnel of a production safe.

Job #3: Fight Choreographer

A fight choreographer (sometimes called a fight director or fight captain) is responsible for safely coordinating stage combat in a production and doing so with absolute safety. Actors are often very inexperienced when it comes to blocked fistfights, knife fights, duels, gunfights, or martial arts sequences, so a fight choreographer must not only teach them basic fight technique, but make sure they don't injure themselves or another actor—and at the same time, make the sequence they're performing look real and convincing to the audience.

Here's a sample list of the fight choreographer's duties:

- Carefully analyzing the script in order to understand the context of fight sequences in the play.
- Working closely with the director to be able to realize his or her vision for fight sequences within the play, and coordinate these sequences within existing blocking.
- Planning, both on paper and through extensive rehearsal, the fight sequences move by move.
- Accident proofing and safety testing all fight choreography once it's been planned.
- Obtaining any props (mock guns, knives, swords, etc.) for the fight sequences.
- Gaining the director's approval by demonstrating the fight choreography.
- Teaching the actors exactly how to execute each step of the fight choreography.
- Teaching the actors how to use any mock weaponry in the fight sequences.
- Making sure the fight choreography appears period correct, if the play takes place in another era.
- Rehearsing the choreography with the actors and being present during the show run to ensure the choreography looks polished and remains safe.
- Jumping into the production to perform the fight choreography if needed (i.e., if a sequence is judged too difficult or complicated for an untrained actor to attempt).

Fight choreographers should have extensive experience themselves as actors and/or dancers, and should be trained in stage combat via a theater arts program. Additional training in martial arts or weaponry is very helpful as well.

Job #4: Scenic Artist

A scenic artist does the hands-on hard work when it comes to executing a set design: he or she paints the set pieces and backdrops to the set designer's specifications. Usually, the scenic artist joins the crew toward the end of a rehearsal period, once the set designer has settled on all the details of how he or she wants the set to look, so often the scenic artist has to work fast, under strict deadlines.

Here's a sample list of the scenic artist's duties:

- Helping the set designer choose paint and supplies if asked.
- Consulting with the set designer regarding the scope, style, texture, and application specifics desired for the look of the painting work.
- Working with set design models or drawings accurately.
- Knowing how to use primer and base coat.
- Knowing how to work with fabrications or wallpaper if necessary.
- Knowing professional brushstroke technique for the best painting results and using economical brushstroke techniques to save time.
- Knowing how to execute specialized painting techniques, like "aging" the look of a set piece.
- Being responsible for fixing mistakes.
- Cleaning up the painting area after every work session.
- Staying available during a show run to touch up the set as needed.
- If you're interested in scenic art, it's true that hands-on experience under the watchful eye of a good designer/ teacher is a great way to get your feet wet. It's also important to study scenic art and design in a theater arts

program, to learn the nuances of the craft, and to be able to put these points into physical practice.

Job #5: Makeup Artist/Wig Designer

A makeup artist/wig designer is responsible for the detailed cosmetic look of an actor in character during a show. This technician creates, in conjunction with the costume designer, character-appropriate hair and makeup styles, then applies or teaches the actor to apply these styles.

Here's a sample list of a makeup artist/wig designer's duties:

- Meet with the director to discuss his/her vision for how makeup and wigs should look within a production.
- Meet with the costume designer to make sure the makeup and wigs can be integrated with the costumes for the production.
- Research any specialized makeup necessary for the production (e.g., period looks or SFX).
- Purchase cosmetics and wigs essential to a production.
- Cut and style wigs to order for each character look.
- Create individual makeup palettes for each actor in the production.
- Teach the actors to apply the makeup themselves, or organize a preshow schedule for applying complex makeup to each actor.
- Teach the actors to don their own wigs, or integrate helping them put on and style their wigs within the preshow schedule.
- Teach actors how to effectively remove theatrical makeup and take off wigs without damaging them.
- Maintain all makeup for cleanliness; clean and restyle wigs daily.
- Restock any makeup supplies that run low.

Makeup artists and wig designers often train in theater arts or fine arts programs and then may be required to take a state license exam before going to work (depending on state regulations). Training in cosmetology and hairstyling is also helpful. One of the great satisfactions of this work? You can help an actor feel comfortable and confident within his or her performance through the accurate look you help them achieve. What a terrific contribution to a production—and to another artist's success!

——————CHAPTER 10 CHECKLIST——————

Get more out of what you've learned in this chapter by:

- ☐ Joining a crew. It's an absolutely mandatory experience for any student interested in any form of theater arts (and often a requirement for a theater arts major, or within a specific course). For the next student or department production at your school, pick the crew job that interests you most first— sign up for costume prep and start sewing and pinning, or choose set prep, grab a brush, and start painting flats. Or grab a spot on a run crew and *really* immerse yourself in the action. Shadow a skilled technician you're interested in who has experience with any of the jobs we've covered, and pitch in wherever you're needed. At the end of that show's run, sign up for an entirely new crew job, and start learning all over again. The more you observe (and try out) different theater jobs, the better you'll understand your own technical strengths and interests. You'll be seasoned, and a lot more informed about the workings of a production, before you know it!

Calling the Show

How are technical effects executed during a performance? They're "called" by the stage manager—an intricate process of set directions over a closed circuit to various show run crew members. This is how lights, sound, and set elements work together within a live production, and is a very intriguing and skill-filled process.

Here's the skinny on the process:

- Everyone on the crew wears a headset, as does the SM; the headsets are wired for group communication.
- The SM will check, person by person, to make sure everyone is "on headset" prior to performance. When you need to take your headset off momentarily, you state you are going "off headset."
- Cue calling terminology:
  - The SM will call a "warning" before a cue is imminent. The crew member responsible for that cue will reply, "Warned."
  - Next, the SM will instruct the crew member to "stand by." The proper reply is "standing" or "standing by."
  - The SM then says "go," and the crew member executes the cue.

Calling cues is a matter of precise timing; usually, about thirty seconds is spaced in by the SM from the time "warning" or "stand by" is called to when the cue should be executed. The SM will get the crew into a good rhythm as rehearsals progress, so the flow of cues will actually start to feel pretty natural eventually.

Teching the Show

"Dry" tech. "Wet" tech. What the heck? These terms may sound pretty weird in the context of final play rehearsals, but they are a vital part of the production process. Here's how these individual processes work:

- **"Dry" tech** is a technical rehearsal without any actors present. Lights, costumes, sets and projections mesh into their final form in these rehearsals. The show's director, lighting designer, sound designer, projection designer, costume designer, technical director, stage manager, props master, master electrician, and technical crew all gather to walk through every second of the show, testing how the effects and costumes look, sound, and feel in real time. All lighting, sound, and projection cues are then written as each technical element is signed off on by the group.
- **"Wet" tech** is when actors are inserted into the technical process and can get a firsthand sense of how the effects will be employed in performance. Often times, wet tech is a slow process as actors are layered in because adjustments to lighting especially often need to be made (a spotlight cue might look different with the actor actually captured by the spot, for instance). Directors often do a lot of tweaking during wet tech, too.

So how is wet tech different than dress rehearsal? Actors don't have to be in costume for wet tech. Often, though, a "costume parade" takes place on the same day as wet tech—actors get partially or fully dressed so the costume designer can check last-minute details under the lights and make any changes required in plenty of time.

11

The Role of the Dramaturg

Expert advice—it's a blessing to have in any situation, of course. But in the throes of putting up a dramatic production, a wise, steady voice that expresses the facts when we need to know them most is invaluable. A good dramaturg fills this spot, bringing knowledge, perspective, and detail to the rehearsal proceedings whenever they're needed.

So what is a dramaturg exactly? It's funny, but many thespians are actually unsure of the precise answer to this question. A good description would be that a dramaturg acts as protector and custodian of the play text, from the time the work is selected for production right through rehearsals and even through the show run period. The dramaturg (who is sometimes referred to as a "literary manager," by the way) is the one person on a show, besides the show's playwright, who understands every theme, intention, and usage of wording on every page of the script. It can even be said that the dramaturg understands more clearly than the playwright what impact the text really has, in that the dramaturg's job is to objectively study the material inside out and make sure its impact and meaning are as clear as possible. To this end, the dramaturg contributes information about the play's details to the director and actors, plus acts as a conduit of information for audience members and students of the text to provide the most accurate experience of the material possible.

How does a dramaturg do this? Through extremely careful overall text study, and thoughtful, word-by-word analysis. Let's break down the dramaturg's duties to get a better understanding of how his or her work is so integral to the play's success as a whole.

SEEKING OUT NEW PLAYS

The dramaturg's first task is to find plays that he or she thinks a theater, or director, would be interested in producing. If the dramaturg works for a company or a university theater program, often new scripts are submitted by playwrights hoping to get their work staged. The dramaturg will read through every script submitted, making copious notes on the quality of each script, usually page by page. Then the dramaturg will usually boil these impressions down into a written evaluation of the play's strengths and weaknesses and determine whether it's good enough to be considered for production. The dramaturg then submits the evaluation to the company, so the company's producer or artistic director can read the play if it's judged to be of quality and interest. The dramaturg may also give an informal verbal evaluation of a play as well.

If a dramaturg works independently for a director, the dramaturg may also be called upon to read and evaluate established plays in a certain genre to help a director decide on a piece to stage. For this reason, freelance dramaturgs often specialize in different subtypes of theater texts, like musical theater or Shakespearean texts.

DIVING INTO THE DETAILS

After a dramaturg presents his or her impressions of a play script to a company or director, the script is, naturally, accepted or rejected for publication. When a script is accepted, it's returned to the dramaturg, whose work starts in earnest at this point.

The dramaturg's primary task at hand is to make this good script even better and perfect it on every level so it's a clear, engaging, and production-friendly piece of material. The dramaturg begins this endeavor by reading the play over and over to understand its themes, points, and scenes as well as technically possible. The dramaturg takes much more detailed notes, most often line by line, during this reading period. The dramaturg also notes any problems or issues that need to be addressed in terms of the script's character development, as well as corrections in logic or pacing when it comes to plot or action within the play.

The dramaturg then makes editing notes: which scenes could use tightening or could be cut altogether? Which lines seem clunky, stiff, or repetitive? The dramaturg can make notes on how these points might be rewritten if that might provide needed clarity, too. Keep in mind, though, that a good dramaturg knows when never to overstep his or her bounds in this regard. A dramaturg should never presume to "improve" on a classic work—heavily editing or attempting to rewrite Shakespeare would obviously be a mistake, and a pretty wild, ego-driven idea to have in the first place. But let's say a dramaturg is working on an original play, with the playwright present during the production process. It's perfectly fine for the dramaturg to bring ideas, suggestions, and impressions to the playwright for consideration in a situation like this. The caveat, though, is that while a dramaturg acts as a skilled adviser, a playwright is the source of the work and therefore is not obligated to take this advice or put any changes into motion that the playwright is opposed to. (For your information: good dramaturgs respect the playwrights and texts they work with, never infringe on a playwright's vision or intention, and are never offended if their suggestions go unheeded.)

That said, a dramaturg's value to a playwright is immeasurable, and a wise writer will definitely take a dramaturg's opinion seriously. When a dramaturg and playwright meet, the dramaturg can give the playwright an unvarnished reality check about the material, which, as any writer knows, is incredibly helpful. The longer a playwright has been thinking about and working on a piece, the less he or she can see it clearly, so having a set of fresh eyes focused on the pages will ferret out problems that the playwright may miss. The playwright will talk extensively with the dramaturg, then study the dramaturg's notes, ultimately decided how to incorporate them into fine-tuning the play (or again, not incorporate them at all). Best-case scenario: the dramaturg and playwright bond over their shared understanding of the play, the playwright grows to trust the dramaturg, and the two work as a fruitful team to make the material the best it can be, in whatever manner that endeavor needs to happen.

ACTING AS A GO-BETWEEN

A dramaturg also serves as an essential conduit between a playwright and a director. How? By maintaining that ever-crucial objective status as protector of the text. If there are disagreements on how to interpret a scene between the writer and the director, the dramaturg can help settle a potential dispute by outlining the objectives of the material clearly, reminding both the writer and director of the reason the scene exists as written, and using that reasoning to foster a compromise and solution. The dramaturg can also attend rehearsals when the playwright can't, help the director with any text questions as blocking and scene work proceeds, and take notes back to the playwright on a daily basis from the director, too. This process saves lots of time and confusion.

During rehearsals, a dramaturg can also take notes and write up constructive criticism when he or she notices that scenes, dialogue, or plot points could use work, now that they can be seen in actual performance. The dramaturg can bring any notes to a director and/or playwright on a daily basis; again, the dramaturg doesn't have the final call in terms of whether these notes make a dent in the production, but if the notes are smart and on point, they will most likely be given some measured thought.

A dramaturg can help the actors in a play, too. During rehearsals, an actor may have questions about his or her character's actions, history, or motivations that are tied directly to the text. With the playwright's blessing, or in the playwright's absence, the dramaturg can skillfully speak to the intention within the play that will shed light and clear up confusion for that actor on the spot. Another helpful tool that a dramaturg often presents an actor with is an information packet. That packet often contains details about the life and times of the character the actor is playing. In a period piece, this information could include geographical info about where the character lived, the occupation of the character, the food the character might eat, popular songs of the era—any nugget, really, depending upon the material itself and the way the production is being staged. For a dramaturg, no such detail is too small to convey.

HELPING OUT WITH THE MARKETING OF A PLAY

A dramaturg's intimate, intricate knowledge of a play can also come in handy for a theater's public relations team. The dramaturg is often consulted for information when it comes to vivid descriptions of characters and plot. This info is then used by the marketing team to colorfully write marketing copy—the dramaturg may also be directly involved in that writing in some cases, too.

PREPARING ACADEMIC MATERIAL

A dramaturg's scholarly understanding of a play is also a natural boon when it comes to assembling educational materials tied to a production. The dramaturg may be called upon to write a comprehensive study guide for a play that tackles a subject from history, for example. The dramaturg will often be the point person as well for any school groups that attend a play's performances. This might entail working with an elementary, middle, or high school teacher to give a preshow talk on the subject matter of the play, answering students' questions so their grasp of the material is as complete as possible when they actually see the play.

FOSTERING AUDIENCE FEEDBACK

After performances, a dramaturg is often given the job of moderating audience feedback sessions as well. Running a question-and-answer session with the playwright, director, and cast, hosting a discussion forum on specific themes in a play, or giving a supplementary talk on topics related to the play—like the overall works of its author, for example—all fall within the scope of a dramaturg's duties.

And what interesting duties they are! If you think you might be interested in a career as a dramaturg, you'll want to study both theater arts and English in college, and take playwrighting classes to boot. You'll need to love logic, read voraciously, write clearly and analytically, and think creatively, too. A dramaturg consistently makes huge and significant contributions to how well a play is understood—and that's worthwhile work indeed.

CHAPTER 11 CHECKLIST

Get more out of what you've learned in this chapter by:

☐ Reading *The Art of Active Dramaturgy* by Leanna Inez Brown (Focus Publishing). A fascinating exploration of the field of dramaturgy—perfect preparation if you might be interested in studying it more intensely or pursuing the craft as a career path.

☐ Evaluating a script for quality. Sit down with the one-act play of your choice and review it for clarity. Take line-by-line notes, asking yourself what makes sense and what needs further clarity. Note your impressions about whether character intentions are clear, if you think the plot makes consistent sense, if the ending of the play is logical and satisfying. Now write up a summary of your impressions and your ideas for how to improve the play wherever you see fit. This is an excellent exercise you can repeat with different plays you read. It will hone your ability to discern a play's quality, sure, but it will also build your confidence in terms of trusting your own opinions and becoming comfortable expressing your intellectual impressions of a dramatic work.

12

Theater Tips and Tricks

Stagecraft is an amazing wonder—you can achieve so much through detailed preparation, hard work, and, as you work on more and more productions, firsthand experience. Yet even the most accomplished thespians around know that things never go *exactly* as you plan onstage. Every theater veteran you speak to will have a war story, or twenty, about the time something awful happened during a show but how quick thinking, company unity, and some practical know-how saved the day. And, invariably, how this unexpected trouble was actually a blessing in disguise, as it taught everyone involved in fixing it that they were smart and capable in the heat of the moment.

Let's talk a bit about theater triage, then. What follows is an analysis of some common theater situations that are unexpected snags at best and emergencies at worst. The good news is that you can survive each of these scenarios and get right back in the saddle with your performances all the wiser. Remember these words of wisdom above all: it's only a play, and you and your company are only human. It's OK to stop, regain control of things, and start again. If your work is good, your audience will forgive any issues, stay engaged with the show, and reward you with extra applause at the end!

Here's what to do when . . .

LINES ARE LOST

Your show's first performance is proceeding perfectly—the scenes are paced smoothly, the audience laughs when you want them to, and your actors are on top of their games. Until . . . one performer totally blanks on her next line. She falls silent and is suddenly wide eyed, unable to remember what words come next for the life of her. Seconds start to tick away. And what's even worse? Lots of times, one actor's slip-up causes a chain reaction of forgotten text by the other actors, either because they panic or because they simply lose their places in the dialogue chain without the correct cue.

Your solution? First of all, let your cast know that if any actor slips up in this manner, it's not the end of the world. Then, for everyone's peace of mind, elect one actor per scene to be ready to riff some lines or reconnect the flummoxed actor back to the scene quickly. This performer could simply say something like "What about the missing cat?" if an actress drops a line about a missing cat, and that will be enough to jog her memory and get the scene moving. Choose an actor who's especially good at improv for this task or an actor who you've noticed is really skilled at thinking on his or her feet. If this doesn't work, and your actress still can't recall her text, it's fine for her to call "Line!" and for the ASM (who should be on-book backstage) to call the line back as a prompt. Obviously you don't want this to be happening all the time during a performance, but I've seen this kind of rescue even on Broadway, and it's really not that big of a deal in terms of breaking continuity.

THE POWER GOES OFF

Carrying on a performance when there's no juice may seem impossible, but you can make things work. Yes, you'll have to give up on lighting and sound cues, but it's really the bones your show is built on that make for quality. Trust that your actors will be at their best, that your play text can stand alone, and that your director's created great staging so your audience will stick with the show.

Practically, you can announce to the audience that the show will go on after a ten-minute intermission—that gives your crew time to check for and deal with any faulty wiring or equipment issues, and call your local power company to confirm an outage. If you find out there's a local blackout (the most common cause of these situations, by the way), open up all the doors to your house to let in as much natural light as possible, and open any drapes or shades over your windows. Locate any battery-powered lighting sources you can—crew members, and even audience members, can train flashlights on your actors en masse! Then just keep going. The sense of accomplishment your company will feel at the end of the show will be immeasurable, and your audience members will greatly appreciate their dedication to making the show go on.

THE SET COLLAPSES

OK, so the bow of your *Titanic* just fell off. It happens! The first thing to do is to make sure that any nearby actors and crew are unhurt. Once you know everyone is OK, ignore the peals of laughter from your audience (there will be at least a few chuckles, and that's OK—it is kind of funny, after all), pause the scene, pull the curtain if you're using one, send out the crew to remove the errant set piece and clean up any debris, and tell your actors to move downstage toward the audience if there's even the slightest risk to anyone's safety by being near the set piece. Then just start the scene from the point it stopped. No drama, no hand-wringing, just get back on track.

A CUE DOESN'T CLICK

Whether a section of the stage fails to light or a sound cue doesn't happen, the smartest decision is always *not* to pause the scene. Your

SM should know to keep his or her crew moving forward through the cue list or confusion can start a snowball effect of lags, or worse, complete disorder if the crew tries to backtrack and play catch-up. Your actors should know not to stop, too.

THERE'S A WARDROBE MALFUNCTION

If an actor's pants fall down, that's embarrassing, but he can survive. The actor should simply pull up his pants, hold them together with his hand, complete his work in the scene, and exit when he normally would to change clothes. If an actress's costume somehow disintegrates and her modesty is at stake, by all means, she should cover herself and discreetly exit, after which the scene can be paused so that she can change quickly. The costume run crew should have a needle and thread stocked in the wings, as well as quick access to substitute pants or shirts for these kinds of emergencies (which don't happen frequently as a rule).

THE CURTAIN WON'T OPEN (OR CLOSE)

If your crew can't manually pull the curtain into the desired position, turn to these fixes. For a curtain that won't open because it's on a malfunctioning winch or pulley, disconnect the drape from this piece of equipment; if it's still stuck on the overhead track, get ladders, and have several crew members lift and drape it over the catwalk or overhead piping, securing it with nails or fasteners. Then just do the performance without a curtain (as well as any set changes—the audience will obviously get the necessity for this). If the curtain won't close, then simply do the show the same way.

AN ACTOR GETS HURT

If the performer's injury is minor—say, he or she gets a small cut on the hand in a fight scene—it's OK for that actor to keep going, as long as he or she is not bleeding (that could be hazardous to other performers in the scene). If there's blood, the scene should be paused, and the actor should head backstage for first aid—your SM and ASM should always keep a basic kit for medical emergencies handy.

If the actor is suddenly overcome with a stomach issue, say from food poisoning, he or should shouldn't soldier on in a scene—that scene should be paused so the actor doesn't actually become sick in front of the audience. And in the case of a serious accident, the show should be stopped, your SM or ASM should call out, "Is there a doctor in the house?," and 911 should be called by a designated crew member.

AN AUDIENCE MEMBER HAS A MEDICAL EMERGENCY

The split second you see or hear about a stricken patron, stop the show. Your SM or ASM should call out, "Is there a doctor in the house?" As in our previous example, a crew member should always be designated to call 911 immediately in this situation. You should also have at least two company members available on the premises who are trained in CPR, and if required by your state (and even if it's not), have a defibrillator on hand at your theater.

THERE'S AN AUDIENCE UPRISING

Say your play tackles a controversial subject. What do you do if your audience doesn't like the play, and walkouts start to occur? First of all, don't be personally offended—art is subjective, as we all know. Plan ahead and decide what your policy on refunding tickets will be, then enact that policy. Listen calmly and respectfully to any complaints patrons may have *outside* the house, so your remaining audience members aren't disturbed. And take from the experience what makes most sense to you. If you think the audience members' criticism has validity, you might want to use it to make adjustments in your show. If you're happy with the work you're presenting, don't change anything. Stick to your message and your vision—you're under no obligation to please anyone, or everyone.

──────────── **SELECTED READING** ────────────

A Crash Course in Special Effects

Stage effects—sure, they're a lot of smoke and mirrors (often literally), but they also often punctuate the most important and memorable moments of a play. A good understanding of SFX (shorthand terminology for stage effects and specialized makeup) is obviously necessary 411 for set designers, lighting designers, sound designers and stage managers—but really, every thespian should have a basic working knowledge of its most-used elements. Why? If you're a director, you need to understand effects capability in order to use them effectively in your production; if you're an actor, you need to understand how to work within an SFX environment safely and convincingly. And so on it goes for each member of a company.

With this need in mind, let's talk a bit about the core principles of stage effects, discuss how some specific visual and aural sleight-of-hand is executed, and, later, take a look at some safe, simple, and surprisingly realistic SFX tricks you can work into your own student productions in a jiff.

Pyrotechnics

Commonly known by its nickname, pyro, these are fire and flame effects. And before we discuss them even a little bit, repeat after me: I will never try these myself. You need a professional licensed and experienced theater technician who specializes in pyro to come in and work these SFX for any production you or your school plans to do. There have been too many stage-related fatal accidents in recent years—you may have heard of the tragic Station nightclub fire in Rhode Island, which was started by pyro SFX—to ever attempt fire and flame effects on your own.

Some of the elements of pyro SFX include the following equipment:

- **Flash pots**—These small mechanical units create on-stage flame visuals and explosions and are safe for usage in a stage space as long as there's proper ventilation and the size of the house is larger than a black box.
- **Smoke pots**—These units create smoke fields that, again, must be executed by a pro in a ventilated space that's larger than a black box.

Strobe Lights

Obviously a stunning visual moment in a production—but again, one that must be executed with extreme caution.

A strobe flashes so quickly that it tricks your brain through its impact on your retina—ultimately, this means any object or stage portion you're looking at appears to be in slow motion. Strobe effects look particularly strong when you drain the stage of ambient lighting; they can be highly effective in scenes where they complement and contrast with actors' movements. Indeed, a wide range of strobe effects can be achieved by using lamps, wash lights, adjustable speed strobe devices, colored strobe devices, circular strobe devices, and rectangular multilight strobe units.

Your lighting designer and lighting techs can operate strobes once they understand how to operate their unit of choice—but they must take care *never* to operate strobes in the presence of any cast or crew members on a production who suffer from epilepsy or another seizure disorder. Strobes can trigger electrical activity in the brain, which could in turn cause potentially life-threatening seizures. So if strobes are to be used in a production, it's imperative not only to protect susceptible company members but also to post clear signs outside your theater warning audience members of their inclusion in the show.

Weaponry

This goes without saying: never use real swords, knives, or, please no, guns onstage! All weapon props should be just that—props—and procured from stage weapon retailers (there are scores of good ones on the web) or from a toy merchandiser, if they read effectively. And remember:

- Any blade you use must have dull or round edges.
- All fake guns must have their barrels blocked. No blanks. It's always best to use a fake gun, some imaginative staging, and a sound effect for the shot.

Squibs

For blood effects, these glorified squirt guns are easy to use—you can buy professional-grade squibs from theatrical prop suppliers. An actor is fitted with a small squib or a squib under a costume piece, and the load of fake blood inside the squib's barrel is activated to blast out through a trigger mechanism. The actor can operate it, or a stagehand can do so remotely. These squib FX rigs are basically a hybrid of a squirt gun and a spud gun. The simple mechanics involve using air to push a load of blood or debris out of a barrel. The air is released with a trigger, activated by a performer or technician nearby. You can also get low-tech and fill small balloons with a mixture of corn syrup and red food coloring, then have the actor squeeze this homemade squib for an oozing visual.

Prosthetics

The sky's the limit in terms of what SFX makeup can accomplish. From aging an actor to making a monster, you can find excellent tutorials on YouTube that demonstrate specific techniques and recommend cosmetic products to get any job done. Let your creativity loose!

────── CHAPTER 12 CHECKLIST──────

Get more out of what you've learned in this chapter by:

Making your own weather SFX.

Here's a no-brainer to start you off: you can flash your stage lighting on and off to create a realistic lightning effect. And if you're looking for good thunderclap sound effects, they're plentiful to choose from on YouTube.

But what about actual precipitation effects—how do you achieve those convincingly? Good news: this kind of SFX is actually much easier than you might think to pull off—and you can safely do it yourself. Here's how to get an eye-popping storm a-brewin' in just a few minutes.

☐ **For an instant blizzard**—Tear up small pieces of tissue, mound them into the shape of flakes, load them into a box with a hole in the bottom, and head up to your catwalk. Shake the snow onto the stage from above, focusing on backlit stage areas for the best visual impact.

☐ **To catch an actor in a snowstorm**—Simple soap suds can be dabbed on hair and clothing to read realistically from the audience.

☐ **To make it rain**—Get a standard-length garden hose, and poke a series of small holes down its length on one side. Attach the hose to a water source, then hang it from the catwalk (fasten it with heavy-duty tape). Turn on the water and you have drizzle. A note of caution: keep water away from any electrical gear.

☐ **To create a full-force rainstorm**—Use the same process above in terms of making rain. Additionally, fill a box with leaves and a lot of uncooked oatmeal, which will look like additional debris in a wind gust. Place high-velocity fans or wind machines on both sides of the stage in the wings; let them blow at the same time you shake the contents of your box onto the stage from the catwalk. A note of caution: water and electricity definitely don't mix, so set your fans to blow in the opposite direction from your water flow, or use battery-powered blowers for your company members' safety.

13

The List
Movers and Shakers Who Shaped Modern Theater

Radical thinking. Technical brilliance. Bold risk-taking. Artistic excellence. These are just a few of the many stunning, influential, and peerless qualities a true theater innovator possesses. We've discussed the work of numerous well-known masters in past chapters, but the following list of creative dignitaries is also very important to familiarize yourself with. These are some of the bravest artists around, in that their vision and talent are wholly original and broke barriers.

These thespians are not afraid to express themselves with complete honesty and transparency—the hallmark traits of a real rule breaker, someone who is willing to stick their neck out and work in a way that brings new insight to an art form. They're the great ones—they changed the face of theater and continue to inspire artists and audiences everywhere.

They follow in no particular order, but with much respect:

Robert Wilson

This virtuoso experimental director also excels as an actor, producer, visual artist, and video/lighting/sound wizard. Wilson's collaboration with composer Philip Glass, *Einstein on the Beach*, is a modern avant-garde touchstone. His additional collaborators included the late Lou Reed, Mikhail Baryshnikov, and Rufus Wainwright. Every detail of Wilson's work, from his chosen stage imagery to the distinctive movements his actors make onstage, has meaning, and that meaning is thrilling.

Tony Kushner

The Pulitzer Prize–winning author of *Angels in America* blew open the doors to vital political discussion in the theater in the 1990s with his compassionate, angry, and determined dissection of the AIDS crisis. Kushner's other acclaimed plays include *Slavs!*, *Homebody/Kabul*, and *Caroline, or Change*; he's also authored the screenplays for Steven Spielberg's films *Munich* and *Lincoln*.

Peter Hall

The former director of London's National Theatre also shaped the agenda of the Royal Shakespeare Company. He helmed many lauded stage productions, including the premiere of *Waiting for Godot*, and wrote a number of seminal books on drama, including the classic *The Necessary Theatre*.

Sam Shepard

Part rock star, part cowboy, all genius. Shepard's body of work as a playwright pushed boundaries and was unfailingly raw, beautiful, violent, and moving. His plays included *True West*, *Buried Child*, *Fool for Love*, *Curse of the Starving Class*, and *Savage/Love*.

Peter Brook

In 1964, Brook directed the first English-language take on *Marat/Sade* with skill and clarity. He was known for his blazingly original versions of *King John* and *Hamlet* and his fruitful collaborations with actors like Paul Scofield.

Andrew Lloyd Webber

A musical miracle man, Webber writes the songs that make the whole world sing. ("Memory" from *Cats*? Check.) His writing partnership with Tim Rice is theater legend; additional credits as a composer include *The Phantom of the Opera, Joseph and the Amazing Technicolor Dreamcoat, Evita, Jesus Christ Superstar,* and *Starlight Express.* Webber's production company, the Really Useful Group, has also used innovative business models to market and stage huge box-office hits in the West End and on Broadway.

Julie Harris

This delicate yet ferociously talented actress made her mark in productions such as *I Am a Camera, The Belle of Amherst, The Lark,* and *Forty Carats,* and is widely recognized as one of the best emotional craftspersons in the history of theater.

Bob Fosse

Fosse's work as a director and choreographer was outrageous, elegant, honest, and smart. Mastering his trademark slinky dance style is aspirational for many performers to this day; his stage classics include *Chicago* and *Sweet Charity,* and his Oscar-winning film work includes *Cabaret* and *All That Jazz.*

Cameron Mackintosh

This prolific producer has a great eye for projects that are both crowd pleasing and artistically excellent. Mackintosh's productions have included *Les Misérables, The Phantom of the Opera, Pippin, Miss Saigon, Cats,* and *Hamilton.*

Sarah Kane

Before her death at just twenty-eight years old, Kane's tragic, extreme writing, which included shocking depictions of violence, both physical and emotional, showed a depth of perception and truth rarely seen in the theater. Her best-known play, *Blasted*, scandalized and challenged audiences with unflinching imagery; among her other highly impactful works were *Phaedra's Love*, *Cleansed*, and *Crave*.

Anna Deavere Smith

Smith, an intellectual and creative force, is arguably the theater's foremost monologist. Her classic work *Twilight: Los Angeles, 1992* freshly examined racial and political mores; she's also known as one of the country's best theater teachers, working with students at New York University, Stanford University, and Carnegie-Mellon.

David Mamet

Mamet's fiery, profane, unvarnished plays are noted for their sharp, searing dialogue and unflinching themes. Taking on topics ranging from financial desperation to sexual harassment, he wrote classics such as *Glengarry Glen Ross*, *American Buffalo*, and *Speed-the-Plow*; artists and audiences wait eagerly for his next works. Mamet also cofounded the highly respected Atlantic Theater Company in New York City.

Robert Brustein

The founder of both Yale Repertory Theatre and the American Repertory Theater, Brustein's academic and insightful approach to achieving dramatic excellence has inspired countless students. Meryl Streep was one of his most famous discoveries as a teacher and mentor. Brustein's book *Letters to a Young Actor: A Universal Guide to Performance* is essential reading.

Glenda Jackson

Completely courageous and memorable onstage, Jackson's indelible work with the Royal Shakespeare Company in London continuously inspired theatergoers and her fellow actors. After winning two Best Actress Oscars for her work in *Women in Love* and *A Touch of Class*, Jackson made a complete career U-turn, becoming a member of Parliament in the UK.

Chita Rivera

Rivera's masterful dancing, acting, and singing lit up shows like *West Side Story*; *Bye, Bye Birdie*; *Chicago*; *Kiss of the Spider Woman*; and *Nine*. She blazed trails for Latino performers in show business, becoming the first Hispanic woman to receive Kennedy Center Honors for her body of work.

Jonathan Larson

Beloved composer of the groundbreaking musical *Rent*, Larson tragically died on the day of its first preview. He was awarded the Pulitzer Prize and three Tonys after his death and remains one of the most respected and studied musical theater forces in modern theater history. His other works included *Tick, Tick . . . BOOM!* and *Superbia*.

Elizabeth Swados

Swados examined the plight of homeless kids in the '70s within the parameters of her classic musical *Runaways*, which set the stage for realism onstage throughout the decades to follow. She also authored politically significant works like *Rap Master Ronnie* and *Doonesbury*.

Jennifer Holliday

Widely hailed as the greatest female singer in the history of musical theater, Holliday first made waves with her formidable stage presence in *Your Arms Too Short to Box with God* at the tender age of nineteen. Two years later, she knocked it out of the park with *Dreamgirls*, originating the role of Effie, for which she won a Tony, and electrifying audiences with her rendition of "And I Am Telling You I'm Not Going." Watch it on YouTube. Right. Now.

Santo Loquasto

A chameleon-like master of visual style, Loquasto has excelled as both a scenic designer and a costume designer, lending his talent to diverse material, from *Hello, Dolly!* to *Bent* to *Grand Hotel* to *Glengarry Glen Ross*.

Michael Bennett

A musical theater master for the ages, Bennett, a dancer, choreographer, composer, playwright, and director, began interviewing aspiring Broadway stars about their lives in the early 1970s. Those interviews became the basis for *A Chorus Line*, Bennett's brilliant, touching theatrical legacy. He also directed the original Broadway production of *Dreamgirls*.

Helen Hayes

"The First Lady Of the American Theater" was known for her immense talent, as well as her pioneering professional success as a savvy female artist at a male-dominated time in the industry. She won an Oscar for her role in the film *Airport*.

Tommy Tune

Tune's affable charm as an actor, singer, and dancer lit up Broadway in productions like *My One and Only*. He also directed crowd-pleasing yet clever productions of *The Best Little Whorehouse in Texas* and *Nine*, and excelled as a forward-thinking producer with a nose for great material.

Audra McDonald

The winner of six acting Tonys—the only performer to claim all four female performance categories—McDonald's soaring soprano has graced productions including *Carousel*, *Master Class*, and *Ragtime*. She crafted the definitive stage portrayal of Billie Holiday in *Lady Day at Emerson's Bar and Grill*, and audiences eagerly await the choice of her next role.

Christopher Durang

Durang's wry, intelligent wit burns through his comedic plays, which include *Sister Ignatius Explains It All for You, Beyond Therapy, Baby With the Bathwater, The Marriage of Bette and Boo*, and *Vanya and Sonia and Masha and Spike*. His best friend and valued collaborator, Sigourney Weaver, has originated many of his characters onstage.

Terrence McNally

McNally writes with moving empathy, often on the struggle for gay rights and the AIDS crisis. His masterful plays include *Corpus Christi, Love! Valour! Compassion!*, and *Lips Together, Teeth Apart*. A courageous and unstoppable figure against creative censorship in any form.

Jason Robards

Robards was a brilliant interpreter of Eugene O'Neill's works; his defining work in plays including *The Iceman Cometh* and *Long Day's Journey into Night* thrilled audiences, and he often collaborated with legendary director José Quintero. A double Oscar winner (for the films *All the President's Men* and *Julia*), Robards was also a military hero, bravely fighting in the navy during World War II.

George C. Wolfe

Wolfe's sensitive yet striking direction of Tony Kushner's *Angels in America* earned universal praise. He also helmed memorable, joyful productions of the musicals *Jelly's Last Jam* and *Bring in Da Noise, Bring in Da Funk* and served as artistic director of the Public Theater in New York City.

Trevor Nunn

Nunn's sweeping, highly emotional directing style perfectly fit his pioneering productions of *Cats, Les Misérables, Sunset Boulevard*, and *Aspects of Love*. He's also an expert reteller of Shakespearean tales, including lauded productions of *The Merchant of Venice*, and is known for his stage collaboration with Ian McKellen.

Jerome Robbins

Many think of Robbins as the father of the modern musical. A graceful, daring and thrilling choreographer and director, Robbins's magic touch beget *West Side Story, The King and I, The Pajama Game*, and *Fiddler on the Roof.*

Des McAnuff

Today's most innovative director when it comes to visually arresting takes on the musical. McAnuff's big, challenging, yet accessible Broadway shows have included *The Who's Tommy, Big River*, and *Jersey Boys.*

Diane Paulus

A colorful visionary, Paulus made her mark with *The Donkey Show*, a raucous, disco-flavored reinterpretation of *A Midsummer Night's Dream* that ran for years in New York and later at the American Repertory Theater in Cambridge, Massachusetts. She then reconceptualized *Pippin*, earning herself a huge Broadway hit that revolutionized theater SFX.

Harvey Fierstein

The gifted Fierstein made an intelligent, humane impression by writing and performing the drama *Torch Song Trilogy*. He went on to lend his writing gifts to *La Cage Aux Folles* and *Kinky Boots*; as one of Broadway's best-loved performers, his credits include Edna in *Hairspray*.

Athol Fugard

This trail-blazing, truth-telling South African playwright's stunning works include *Master Harold . . . and the Boys, The Road to Mecca*, and *Tsotsi*. An outspoken anti-apartheid activist, Fugard's culturally and politically important works are performed throughout the world; the Fugard Theatre in Capetown is his legacy's home.

Patti LuPone

Throwing off star quality in abundance, LuPone established her brilliance as a singer and actress in the 1978 Broadway production of *Evita* and later originated the role of Fantine in *Les Misérables*. In recent years, she's given big, dazzling performances on the Great White Way in *Gypsy* and *War Paint*.

Kevin Kline

A Renaissance man of the theater, Kline can do it all: he's a masterful song-and-dance man who thrilled audiences in *On the Twentieth Century* and *The Pirates of Penzance*, as well as a skilled interpreter of Shakespeare, as he proved in *Henry IV*. A skilled comedian, he not only won the 2017 Tony for *Present Laughter* but also won an Oscar for his hilarious, original turn in *A Fish Called Wanda*.

Zero Mostel

A comedic powerhouse whose fantastic work stands the test of time, Mostel crafted perfect performances on Broadway in *Fiddler on the Roof* and *A Funny Thing Happened on the Way to the Forum*. Sympathetic, kind, fiery, boisterous, and wise all at the same time, his talent can be enjoyed fully in the 1968 film version of *The Producers*.

Gregory Hines

Hines was one of the theater's finest dancers, known for his magical tap skills, as well as his graceful, knowing work as an actor. He distinguished himself as a unique, sterling force in the Broadway hits *Eubie!*, *Jelly's Last Jam*, and *Sophisticated Ladies*. Hines's jaw-dropping dance duet with Mikhail Baryshnikov in the film *White Nights* is a must-see.

Nathan Lane

One of the most popular and versatile actors in the theater, Lane moves seamlessly between excellent musical roles and probing dramatic parts. His stellar credits include *The Producers*, *Laughter on the 23rd Floor*, *A Funny Thing Happened on the Way to the Forum*, and *The Frogs*; as a skilled interpreter of the work of Terrence McNally, Lane also earned acclaim in plays such as *Lips Together, Teeth Apart*.

Zoe Caldwell

A firebrand of talent, Caldwell's mastery of theater performance as an art form has encompassed roles in *Othello*, *Vita and Virginia*, and *Master Class*, in which she embodied Maria Callas with humor, intimidation, and pure heart. Many young actors rightfully consider her work to be the gold standard.

Jessica Tandy

Tandy's portrayal of Blanche DuBois in *A Streetcar Named Desire* wowed the theater community with its lack of vanity and abundance of honesty. She went on to perform memorable roles in productions like *The Gin Game* and *Foxfire*, often working with her husband Hume Cronyn. Her beautiful performance style shines in her Oscar-winning lead role in the film version of *Driving Miss Daisy*.

Stephen Sondheim

The god of musical theater, period. Sondheim's lilting, lovely, melodically intricate compositions in *Merrily We Roll along*, *Company*, *Into the Woods*, *Assassins*, *Sunday in the Park with George*, and scores of other shows define the art form as we know it. His work feels like pure magic when you experience it—the ultimate quality only a true original can conjure.

──────── CHAPTER 13 CHECKLIST ────────

Get more out of what you've learned in this chapter by:

- ☐ Watching any of the work of these incredible artists. YouTube is, of course, a rich resource of performance archives, especially from the Tony Awards.

- ☐ Watch Fosse's *All That Jazz* in its entirety. The film is an incredibly realistic depiction of the New York theater world, from the thankless cattle-call audition sequence that opens the movie, to the obsessive, workaholic style of its fictitious director, played beautifully by Roy Scheider.

14

Theater Companies
That Count

A theater company is a living, breathing testament to the dreams, ideas, and innovative thinking of its members. When a group of artists shares a vision and puts that vision into motion with commitment, determination, and hard work, incredible achievement takes place. There's nothing more exciting than finding your creative kindred spirits and going on a ride together.

What follows is a capsule collection of ten theater companies blazing trails across today's performance landscape. They're each established, respecting, courageous artistically, and constantly reinventing the wheel in terms of the quality and ambition of their stage work. Read on to discover why each of these companies inspires artists the world over, and feel free to model your work on their audacious models.

Steppenwolf Theater Company (Chicago, Illinois)

In 1974, high school buddies Gary Sinise and Jeff Perry started a revolution in January in Highland Park, Illinois, with Perry's college friend Terry Kinney. The three staged a lauded production of *And Miss Reardon Drinks a Little*; encouraged by the positive reaction, they followed up with *The Glass Menagerie* and *Rosencrantz and Guildenstern Are Dead*. By 1975, their company, named Steppenwolf, was established as a permanent entity, and future stars including John Malkovich and Laurie Metcalf joined the group. Throughout the '80s, Steppenwolf earned a reputation as one of the country's preeminent homes for vivid, realistic works, from Sam Shepard plays to *The Grapes of Wrath*. Now forty-four members strong, Steppenwolf has won scores of Tonys and the National Medal of Arts, and is universally recognized as one of the world's finest theater ensembles.

Williamstown Theater Festival (Williamstown, Massachusetts)

Since its founding by the news director of Williams College, Ralph Renzi, and the college's drama director, David C. Bryant, the Williamstown Theater Festival has set the standard for excellence when it comes to resident summer companies. Bradley Cooper, Gwyneth Paltrow, Christopher Reeve, Nathan Lane, Frank Langella, and Christopher Walken are just a few of the luminaries who have performed at Williamstown, which was guided by executive artistic director Nikos Psacharopoulos for more than three decades. The material the company tackles spans the work of Tennessee Williams, George Bernard Shaw, and Tom Stoppard; has transferred numerous productions to Broadway; and earned a Tony in 2002.

The Wooster Group (New York, New York)

A much-admired touchstone of modern experimental theater. The impetus for Wooster Group blossomed out of work done by members of New York's entity the Performance Group during the mid-70s. By 1980, director Elizabeth LeCompte had taken a leadership role, and the Wooster Group was officially formed; among the founding members was LeCompte's partner at the time, Willem Dafoe. The troupe got its name from its neighborhood location, Wooster Street in Soho, and soon grew to include nearly thirty associate members, including Frances McDormand.

The Wooster Group's approach is to spin classic texts in a new way, infusing Shakespeare with radical and fascinating performance techniques, sound recordings, and video technology. An unfailingly fearless and forward-thinking company!

Punchdrunk (London, UK)

Founded by director/designer Felix Barrett, Punchdrunk specializes in exhilarating, site-specific theater. Its most famous production, *Sleep No More*, is an adaptation of *Macbeth* that has been staged in both an old school building and a hotel; audience members walk from room to room, essentially dropping in on scenes at will, or following actors they are interested in watching. Additional interactive productions have been performed at London's National Maritime Museum, an old army installation, a forest complete with a mystical mansion, tunnels, and a distillery. Punchdrunk productions contain very little if any dialogue, and rely on interaction to move their stories forward.

The ultimate immersive experience.

LAByrinth Theater Company (New York, New York)

Run by the late legendary actor Philip Seymour Hoffman and John Ortiz for many years, and subsequently led by costume designer Mimi O'Donnell, LAByrinth was founded in 1992 by a collective of thirteen actors as a show of mutual support. Each member would get the chance to act, plus write, direct, produce, do tech—the company was a complete artistic democracy from day one. Distinguished company members also include Ellen Burstyn, Bobby Cannavale, Chris Rock, Ethan Hawke, and playwright Cusi Cram. The company's hallmark is honest, original work dealing with diverse ethnic issues and urban life.

The Actors' Gang (Los Angeles, California)

Founded by Oscar-winning actor and director Tim Robbins, The Actors' Gang has produced over 150 plays since the 1980s. Social relevance is a recurring theme in the company's work; members include Jack Black, John Cusack, and Helen Hunt.

The company works within the California prison system to encourage inmates to develop social skills and self-esteem through theater involvement. The Actors' Gang also pioneered "the style," a new acting method that combines commedia dell'arte, mask performance, and emotional development that is subsequently used in performance to help an actor realize new possibilities as a creative artist.

The New Group (New York, New York)

The New Group and its founder, esteemed director Scott Elliott, is dedicated to the quality interpretation of contemporary plays. The company's productions have included *This Is Our Youth*, *Hurlyburly*, *Ecstasy*, and *A Lie of the Mind*, and the New Group developed the now-classic musical *Avenue Q*. Members include Peter Dinklage, Michelle Williams, Paul Dano, Matthew Broderick, Jennifer Jason Leigh, Ed Harris, Cynthia Nixon, and Mark Ruffalo.

Woolly Mammoth (Washington, DC)

An attitude of fun and creative adventure fuels Woolly Mammoth, which was founded in 1980 by Howard Shalwitz, Roger Brady, and Linda Reinisch. The company specializes in plays that are political in nature but inclusive of both liberal and conservative points of view. Woolly Mammoth's production history includes work by playwrights Doug Wright, Tracy Letts, David Lindsay-Albaire, and Sarah Ruhl.

The Mischief Theatre (London, UK)

Helmed by artistic director Henry Lewis and company director Jonathan Sayer, the Mischief's excellence at staging improvised shows is peerless and is widely admired throughout the theater community in

Europe. Starting with the hit production *Let's See What Happens* in 2008, the Mischief has staged *Lights! Camera! Improvise!*, *Improvaganza*, and *The Murder before Christmas*, among other tongue-in-cheek, fun shows.

The company's most renowned production, *The Play That Goes Wrong*, toured internationally and settled in for a successful run in the West End; it dealt with a drama group trying to put on a show that goes hilariously awry during every single scene. *The Comedy about a Bank Robbery*, another Mischief smash, is playing in the West End at the time of this writing. The company's holiday comedy *A Christmas Carol Gone Wrong* was adapted for the BBC, and starred Derek Jacobi and Diana Rigg.

Arts in the Armed Forces (New York, New York)

Cofounded by film and television actor Adam Driver, a former marine, Arts in the Armed Forces brings live theater to US military bases all across the globe. The company gears its work toward active military members, veterans, and their civilian family members, with a view toward opening up communication and solving social issues. To this end, each production concludes with a question-and-answer session between audience and playmakers and time set aside for theatergoers to meet the show's cast. As with all of the companies we've just learned about, Arts in the Armed Forces strives to make a difference, not only onstage but also in its viewers' perspectives—the core goal of all important theater work.

─────── **CHAPTER 14 CHECKLIST**───────

Get more out of what you've learned in this chapter by:

☐ Watching *Of Mice and Men*, the 1992 film adaptation of
Steppenwolf's brilliant stage version of John Steinbeck's
novella. Directed by Gary Sinise and starring Sinise as
George and John Malkovich as his brother Lennie, and
with effective supporting turns by Joe Morton and Sherilyn
Fenn, this tragic, moving story is a great example of
Steppenwolf's hallmark work. It's powerfully unflinching
in its depiction of struggle and pain, but shines a deeply
sympathetic light on its characters despite their flaws and
offers a tenuous sense of hope to its audience throughout.

15

Creative Courage

If you ask almost any thespian to honestly admit what they are most worried about when it comes to taking part in a play, the honest answer, invariably, will be, "What if I'm not good enough?" The most experienced actors, directors, playwrights, and even producers struggle with this kind of self-doubt, so you can imagine what a student brand-new to dramatic expression is dealing with. Maybe you're dealing with it as you read these very words. You have a scene coming up in class you have to act in; you're worried about making a mistake and having your classmates and teacher judge you. You love the experience of having a one-act you've written staged at your school—but what if the jokes in it fall flat because you didn't perfect them quite enough?

It's understandable to feel nervous and dubious about the mere thought of theatrical participation. No one wants to fail, first of all. And the theater is such an emotional enterprise: you're conjuring up joy, pain, anger, and every other feeling in the rainbow. You're revealing yourself in any work you perform, direct, or write. If you're an actor, you need to be physically uninhibited as well to express a character fully. No wonder you've got some butterflies! What can make you even more reticent is having had past experience with rejection, too, not only in the realm of your life, but maybe onstage if you've dipped your toe into drama before. "Constructive" criticism can often sting and sometimes leave an unwarranted mark on your psyche for years to come.

You can get past all of this, though, and find your creative courage. Really, you can. It's a step-by-step process, and it takes a little practice to get right. So start today! Walk yourself through the following ten steps before you head to class, rehearsal, or performance, then make a habit of going through this list before every theater work session from this day forward. Soon, these bravery-building tips will start to subconsciously dismantle your creative anxiety and clear your perspective. You'll feel a sense of control, knowing you alone are responsible for your reactions to other people's opinions of your work. You'll also see that you can create your own theatrical identity, any way you want to! You can improve on any part of your technique the way you like as well: you can rehearse your lines more often, read more books on directing, rewrite a problematic scene over and over until it feels right. Or you can feel free *not* to improve any aspect of your work that you're already satisfied with. Creative courage simply means that you're not afraid to trust the power of your own judgment. And when your own judgment counts most, you have no fear—and you do wonderful work.

Here are your steps. Get ready to feel brave and free!

☐ Embrace your nerves. Admitting you're nervous means you're facing the fact that you need to do something to chill. Just tell yourself, "OK, I'm nervous. Let's do something about that."

☐ Calm your mind. It's a cliché, but it works: spend one minute thinking about your "happy place." Think of one of your favorite spots in the world—in a forest, on a beach, in your room at home, wherever you feel most comfortable. Let feelings of peace and stillness flow through you as you imagine the beautiful details of this place.

☐ Breathe right. Four consecutive deep breaths in, then out, change your physical and mental perspectives dramatically. You relax involuntarily, too. It's that simple.

☐ Drill, drill, then drill some more. Set aside time for one more quick rehearsal of whatever theatrical task you're anxious about. The more you rehearse it, the more it becomes second nature, and you'll have nothing to worry about.

☐ Rehash your victories. Think back to accomplishments in your life that made you proud. Let the good feelings of those memories wash over you right before you begin your task, and you'll feel great about your abilities.

☐ Talk to a mentor. Get your feelings out to a trusted teacher, your mom or dad, a friend, or a counselor. Just talking about your worries can really relieve your mind.

☐ Take a compliment. When you talk to that trusted person, *believe* it when he or she tells you about how talented you are (and they'll tell you that, I bet). It's hard to see yourself objectively. It makes sense that if someone you think is wise tells you that you're a good actor, you're a good actor, doesn't it? So gratefully accept their praise and know you're a good actor from here on out.

☐ Get a lucky charm. Sounds crazy, but tucking a penny you found into your pocket or wearing your "magic" red socks can't help but give you a little confidence boost. I mean, it couldn't hurt.

☐ Practice positivity. Make a decision before performing your task that no matter what happens, it's all good. At the least, you're getting a chance to perform, or write or direct, and that will help you grow. At best, you're gonna hit this scene right out of the park!

☐ Remember why you're here. Because you've grown to love theater. Or you were born loving theater. Because you want to express yourself. And because you're a liver of life, and theater makes you feel alive. That's worth taking a chance on, and doing the best work that you can do!

SELECTED READING

Engaging Acting Exercises

An actor's currency is owed to the ease with which he or she can communicate emotions, intentions, and logic within any given scene. And the instrument an actor has to work with? Quite obviously, it's his or her body. That's why being comfortable with your physical self as a performer is a totally essential skill that must be perfected. Easier said than done, though. As we've discussed, who among us doesn't feel shy, inhibited, or reticent when it comes to moving our bodies in real life from time to time? Now imagine doing so onstage. We might feel awkward, clumsy, or silly in a situation where our physical expressions are on display for all the world to see (read: and make fun of).

As a layperson, you might think that being in character onstage would go a long way to helping an actor feel more comfortable with physical movement or expression, and that's a logical concept. In the earliest stages of an actor's experience, though, it's hard to fully "lose" oneself, so even while in character, an actor may be internally monitoring his or her physical movements and expressions—effectively judging his or her own performance and appearance more harshly than an audience ever could. We call this observing with your "third eye," and for a performer, it can be pretty deadly as far as true creative immersion is concerned. This is where a good acting exercise (or several) can work wonders. Wise actors at every stage of their artistic careers learn, hone, and rely upon a variety of acting exercises to serve various elements of their physical skill set, from relaxation to shedding self-imposed inhibitions to improving listening and speaking skills.

Let's take a closer look at a series of tried-and-true exercises designed to open up an actor to a fuller command of his or her body as a creative tool.

Utilizing These Exercises as a Set

The set you're about to learn consists of eight exercises; they're easy to learn and easy to do but are very valuable. You should do these exercises as a series, at the start of a rehearsal or class, to prepare your body for the physical work you'll be doing as you act—essentially, as a warm-up. Work with your classmates, preferably by gathering in a circle. These exercises are intended to be performed in order, with the following goals in mind:

- To relax your body: two exercises
- To positively energize your body: two exercises
- To encourage physical communication between yourself and your fellow actors: two exercises
- To explore and cement trust between yourself and a fellow actor: two exercises

Once you've completed the exercises in order, you should feel ready and raring to act! The entire set will take about fifteen minutes.

Exercises, in Order

Relaxation Phase

Tense and Relax

Lie flat on the floor of your classroom or stage. Focus your attention completely on your toes. Tense the muscles in each toe as tightly as you can for a count of ten. Next, fully relax your toes, being present in the feeling of this release for ten seconds. Next, move up to the rest of your feet; focus, tense the muscles in your feet for ten seconds, then relax the same muscles for ten seconds. Now, move up to your ankles, doing the same. Repeat all the way up your body—knees, hips, stomach, chest, shoulders, neck, facial muscles. By the time you've tensed and relaxed each muscle group this way, you'll feel loose, calm, and ready to express yourself.

Big Breathing

"Big" breathing means taking large, deep inhalations from your diaphragm, then exhaling them—a physical process that calms every portion of your body almost instantly. Sit in a chair, letting your arms dangle by your sides, and relaxing your legs straight in front of you. Now, take a deep breath in at your core, focusing your effort at the center of your diaphragm. Hold the breath for a count of four, then exhale deeply for another count of four. Repeat ten times.

Energizing Phase

The Big Shake

Everyone in your group extends their right hand and shakes it vigorously for a count of ten. Repeat with the left hand for a count of ten, the right arm for a count of ten, the left arm for a count of ten, the left leg for a count of ten, the right leg for a count of ten, and then a vigorous hip shake (like using a hula hoop) for a count of twenty.

Just Jump!

In unison, your group does ten jumping jacks. On the jump up, everyone yells "Just!" and upon landing, yells "Jump!" as loudly as possible. At the end of the ten jacks, count to ten as a group, keeping your vocal energy high and loud! Now repeat ten more jacks. Then another ten count. Then a last repeat of ten more jacks.

Physical Communication Phase

Emotional Output

Each actor should turn to face the actor next to him/herself. A teacher or leading group member shouts out an emotion—"Happy!" or "Sad!" or "Scared!" or "Confused!"—and at each command, you and your partner express this emotion with your face and body for three seconds. Your teacher or leading group member should shout out twenty different emotions to complete the exercise.

Listening—*Really* Listening

A revved-up, grown-up version of that classic childhood game "Telephone." Gather into a circle. Your teacher or leading group member clearly whispers a random sentence in the ear of a student—it should contain a person, possession, and place (like "Helen took her poodle to Westchester"), avoiding familiar, well-known, or obvious phrases. The student then whispers it to the student next to him/her, and so on, till it goes around the circle. The first round of the game should work successfully, in that everyone repeats the phrase accurately (the last student repeats it aloud to the group). Next round, though, the teacher should state a new phrase with an extra word, an adverb (like "Joe swiftly rode his bicycle to Hastings-on-Hudson"). Go around the circle again, this time more quickly; it'll be a little harder to clearly hear and repeat this time. Third round: the teacher should state a list consisting of ten diverse words at a breakneck pace. As the circle repeats the list, each student will need to concentrate and listen intensely at a new pace in order to accurately articulate the words. Repeat this entire exercise again, encouraging students to focus as intently as possible on each word they hear.

Trust Phase

Liftoff

Partner with another student of your own approximate height and size. Stand heel to heel, back-to-back, holding hands. One student leans forward, and the other leans back against that student. The forward-leaning student controls the motion as you sway forward and backward ten times, On the eleventh count, the forward-leaning student lifts the other student slightly off the floor. The passive student allows him- or herself to be balanced, maintaining a relaxed and trusting posture. Now switch and repeat.

The Safe Fall

Partner with another student. Have two additional students serve as safety spotters, standing behind each of you. Face your partner. He or she should hold his or her arms out, and you allow yourself to fall forward into his or her arms. Repeat twice, then switch. Next, repeat the exercise falling backward (this time, your safety spotters should support your partner's weight from beyond to ensure no one gets hurt). The result? True physical freedom, bonding, and a new sense of confidence—what every actor needs.

────── CHAPTER 15 CHECKLIST ──────

Get more out of what you've learned in this chapter by:

☐ Keeping a dramatic activity journal. Each day, after you write a scene, direct some blocking, or perform a monologue in class, write down all of your feelings about the experience you had. Ask yourself how you felt before, during, and after your work. Note the feedback you received from your teacher, classmates, or audience members who were present. Record the mistakes you think you made, the accomplishments you made in your work, and what you learned from your experience. End each entry by writing a sentence about what you did best—as in, "I spoke much more clearly as I recited my lines" or "I felt great about the performances I guided my actors to." At the end of each week, reread your entries—you'll see forward motion and progress! Your confidence will start to build as you clearly track the hard work that goes into mastering your theatrical skill set and as you see and feel your work improving every single day.

PART THREE

Putting Your Knowledge into Practice

16

A New Way to Watch a Play

Throughout this book, we've discussed the intricate elements of a theatrical production in depth; at this point, it's safe to say you understand the mechanics by which a play is conceived, staged, and performed. Congratulations! So, what should you do with this intellectual and creative information? Put it into practice by watching a play in a whole new way, using your critical thinking skills.

Now, maybe you haven't seen a whole huge number of plays to begin with. That's perfectly OK. You don't have to feel intimidated at the thought of analyzing a piece of theater with little experience, even after reading this book up to this point and taking a theater class. What you glean when you see a play is very individualized; it's a highly personal experience. You know what you like, and you know what you don't like; own those things. Trust your instincts. If you think a scene is sloppily directed, that's a valid opinion. If you love the way dialogue in a scene seems to sing out emotionally, terrific, you're right! Your experience is totally true for you and should be absolutely respected (by you and by everyone else, for that matter).

That said, let's start this exercise by identifying your goal as cementing your impression of the play you are about to choose to see. This means that when you go in to the performance, you aim is simply to review the elements of the play and ask yourself whether you feel these elements were executed well and properly. What really worked? What's lacking? How would you have improved the production or the material itself at its core? The more questions you ask and answer, the more your evaluation ability will strengthen and the more comfortable you'll feel in trusting your own artistic judgment. Which can lead to more wonderful things, like giving you the impetus to become a playmaker yourself (or maybe a very wise and discerning theater critic).

Here's your step-by-step guide for viewing a play through this new lens. The following twenty points will make the process simple and clear to accomplish and give you a map to follow mentally every time you watch a play in the future (the more theater you watch, the more these points will become ingrained in your subconscious). You can use this guide while watching virtually any type of theatrical production—from an educational show to a small, professional showcase to a big Broadway extravaganza, whatever strikes your interest. Here we go!

1. Choose a play you find truly interesting. Make sure it's by a playwright you respect, features an actor you admire, or deals with subject matter you find interesting or personally identify with. That way, your attention will stay engaged as you watch.

2. I recommend choosing a seat about four rows from the stage, dead center in the row if you can swing it. This will give you the clearest view in terms of a comfortable distance to take in the entire stage tableau and will provide good acoustics, too. Of course, any seat you're comfortable

in works, too—if you'd prefer an aisle seat or love hanging out in the balcony, do what feels best to you in terms of location.

3. See the play by yourself if possible (don't feel socially awkward about it, either—lots of folks go to the theater solo!). This will help you concentrate on every point of the play without being distracted by conversing with a friend or date. If you do end up going to the play with a companion, make sure this person knows you're evaluating it so that they respect your concentration.

4. Bring a pad and pen with you to note your impressions, and to jot down answers to the following questions.

5. When the play begins, do you feel the initial blocking works with the text being delivered? Is the stage movement too busy, too static, or right on the money?

6. Does the audience appear engaged in the action from the start of the play? Are they leaning forward in their seats with interest, or do people look bored?

7. Which actors do you feel are the most compelling? Are there any performers you find unconvincing? Note why you have these impressions.

8. Is the lighting enhancing or distracting? Is it too dark or bright?

9. Does the set create a "world" onstage, or does it look out of place in terms of the environment the play exists within? Do set pieces look cheesy or inappropriate in any way?

10. Are the costumes accurate in terms of period and in terms of depicting the essence of each of the play's characters?

11. Are there any obvious technical mistakes, or does every cue, set change, and SFX run smoothly?

12. Can you hear the actors well as they project their voices? If there are sound effects in the play, are they jarring or

too loud, or are they integrated well into the play's dialogue and scene shifts?

13. Does the text make sense if you are watching an original play? If you're watching a well-known play, are the basic points of each scene conveyed clearly via the direction and performances?

14. Are you looking at your watch yet? Your attention should be firmly rooted in the action onstage if the work is good.

15. Do you feel that each scene moves the play's action forward to a new point? Can you clearly connect these dots in terms of a well-paced feeling of momentum, or do you find that some scenes feel draggy?

16. Are there any moments you feel are just plain silly, clunky, or otherwise cringe worthy? Why do these obvious nonworking moments fail, specifically?

17. Do you feel the text makes sense overall?

18. Does the conclusion of the play feel logical, or do any elements feel like they came out of nowhere or were not true to the essence of the play as a whole?

19. What did you learn while watching the play? Was a particular performance illuminating in terms of the actor's technique? Were you impressed by the way a scene transition was handled, in that it was effectively fresh? How did the play add to your theatrical knowledge?

20. If you didn't like a particular element of the play, do you think there was an objective reason why (i.e., the work was not executed properly in terms of stagecraft in some way), or was your reaction emotional and visceral? All feelings are acceptable, so even if the play was done well, if you didn't respond to it, so be it.

21. Did you feel alive when watching the play? Good theater makes you feel vital! If you felt you were a part of the performance—in that you were moved, thrilled, angry, sad, intellectually challenged, or technically wowed—you've

been infused with the magic of live performance. No play is perfect—but the best ones are inclusive, evoke our deepest impulses, and leave us thinking deeply. Hopefully, you just had that incredible and unique experience!

SELECTED READINGS

Ten of the World's Coolest Theater Spaces

One of the most amazing facts you'll ever learn about theater is that it can be done anywhere. In a house with a large stage. In a black box with a tiny stage. In an open-air field. In a parking lot. Where there's a will, and a sense of adventure and imagination, there's a way to put up a show—and the more unusual, neat or unconventional the performance spirit is, the more fascinating the experience of watching a play can be.

There are scores of glorious theaters all around the world. You can find historic, beautiful structures; in-the-round facilities; state-of-the-art, cutting-edge facilities; or quaint, drafty little holes in the wall. They're all valid and always a treat to discover. As you see more and more plays, you'll no doubt experience a variety of theater space styles, and, hopefully, you'll enjoy exploring each and every one of them. For a true fan of architecture, structure, and interior/exterior beauty, though, nothing beats a trip to one (or more) of the world's most unique theater spaces. Your itinerary—either in terms of planning for an upcoming theater visit or simply a journey to put on your bucket list—starts right here and right now!

Let's walk through ten of the world's coolest theater spaces. They're very diverse in terms of history, geography, audience capacity, and detail, but each space is beautiful and creatively life changing to behold in its own way. Please note that this list is far from exhaustive—there are so many other wonderful spaces to appreciate around the world as well. So why did I focus specifically on these ten? They each have a unique ambience that truly flavors the work being produced on their stages—the vibe of each space inhabits a play's text, and feels like the perfect setting to the work produced within its confines. That's the ideal definition of a great theater space to me: a place for homecoming. The space should welcome home the right play, welcome home audience members who instantly feel comfortable there, and welcome home great art as a whole. These spaces get that concept just right.

The Delacorte Theater (Central Park, New York, New York)

Round into Central Park from Eightieth Street in Manhattan, head for the Great Lawn, and you'll find yourself instantly immersed in illustrious theater history. You'll be at the Delacorte, the hallowed site of the Public Theater's summertime staple programming, Shakespeare in the Park. Since its founding in 1962, the Delacorte has welcomed over five million audience members to nearly two hundred free productions.

Every season, two productions are slated, one of which is a Shakespeare piece, and the second of which is often another classic work, such as a play by Brecht or Chekhov. Theatergoers take a place in line early on a hot summer morning and happily wait throughout the day to earn one of that evening's 1,872 seats. Then, as dusk descends over the park, everyone settles in to watch legendary actors like Meryl Streep, Natalie Portman, Anne Hathaway, and Al Pacino tread the boards.

The Delacorte is a completely open-air space, with Central Park's well-loved Turtle Pond and the gorgeous Belvedere Castle visible behind its stage. This adds to the atmosphere of each production immensely. The wildlife surrounding the Delacorte performance area is also sometimes (unintentional) entertainment—a raccoon or two have been known to actually wander across the front of the stage during shows. (Performers learn to take these little onlookers in stride, by the way.)

Sydney Opera House (Sydney, Australia)

Resembling a series of elegant seashells against the waterline of Sydney Harbor, the Sydney Opera House is one of the most iconic and striking theatrical structures ever built. The Opera House's distinctive white and cream concrete circular units are constructed on large podiums that rest on 588 concrete piers—the piers are sunk up to 82 feet below sea level. Glass panels and pink granite make up the house's exterior walls, and a beautiful stone-laid forecourt and extravagant steps further complement the structure's vast beauty.

Inside, the house's performance spaces include its Concert Hall, a 2,679-seat venue with a ten-thousand-pipe organ; the Joan Sutherland Theatre, a proscenium venue that seats 1,507; the Dram Theatre, seating 544 and home to the prestigious Sydney Theatre Company; a 398-seat playhouse; and a 400-person-capacity studio space.

The public is given great access to every corner of the Sydney Opera House—guided backstage tours give a daily glimpse into the workings of the theater as it readies for performances. A recording studio, restaurants, a shopping area, and conference facilities are also available to enjoy.

The Seebühne (Lake Constance, Austria)

Taking the idea of a theater house on the water to an even greater extreme, the Seebühne actually built its stage, and subsequently each of its sets, directly atop glassy Lake Constance; playgoers sit directly on the lake as well. Built in 1946, the Seebühne boasts 6,800 seats.

Stunning stage tableaus with the night sky as a backdrop adds to the drama of watching a play or opera performance at the Seebühne. The theater was the site of a key sequence in the James Bond film

Quantum of Solace and is home to the yearly Bregenz Festival. A truly one-of-a-kind site.

Cutler Majestic Theater (Emerson College, Boston, Massachusetts)

Constructed in 1903, the Majestic was quickly dubbed "the House of Gold" for its abundance of gold leaf detailing. The Majestic's design was inspired by the Palace of Versailles. The theater boasts incredible flourishes, such as red marble Roman columns, fruit and flower garland, decorative cherubs, grape leaves, and elaborate wall sculptures, all elements of the beaux arts design style.

The Majestic is noted for its excellent acoustics and has completely unobstructed views from all seats (it was built without pillars for this purpose). It's the perfect venue for many and varied professional opera, dance, and theater performances, and an incredible asset for Emerson's students to utilize as part of their arts education.

The *Cutty Sark* Michael Edwards Studio Theatre (London, UK)

The historic *Cutty Sark* ship is on permanent display for daily tours in London—but the most intriguing part of its public availability may be the highly unusual fact that a working theater is nestled in its lower hold. Indeed, the Michael Edwards Studio Theatre, which now resides in what was the *Cutty Sark*'s main cargo place, holds an eclectic selection of after-hours performances season after season. From its pre-Edinburgh comedy festival to performances from the acclaimed Trinity Laban Conservatoire, this 103-seat venue is warm, cozy, and incredibly atmospheric—note that its perimeter is packed with authentic antique tea chests.

Cherry Lane Theatre (New York, New York)

The Cherry Lane has survived a long string of different incarnations. Ensconced on Commerce, a curvy side street in Greenwich Village, it's been a brewery, a tobacco warehouse, a box factory. Encompassing a generous 1,200-square-foot space, the Cherry Lane also contained a restaurant in the 1950s and became a nightclub in the 1960s. When the building next door was excavated, an underground river, packed with turtles, was even discovered on the premises.

As a playhouse, the Cherry Lane has featured the talents of Barbra Streisand, James Earl Jones, Joseph Chaikin, Harvey Keitel, Frank Langella, Gene Hackman, F. Murray Abraham, and Lee Strasberg, to name just a small list of luminaries. The building's Old World charm has been carefully preserved, and a sixty-seat studio space was added in 1998. A great place to experience old-fashioned city warmth and excellent modern performance offerings.

The Cuvilliés Theatre (Munich, Germany)

This horseshoe-shaped space consists of four floors, dappled in red and gold. It boasts the electoral loge, the center artistic space of the room, surrounded by atlases. The boxes that surround the loge speak to the historic class system in Germany. Specifically, audience boxes for nobility on the theater's highest level are very ornate; then descending to the third, second, and ground floor, the decorative elements of the Cuvilliés gradually taper off to plain furnishing. A great place to observe tradition, as well as see today's best theater performers.

Marjorie Walter Goodhart Theater (Bryn Mawr College, Montgomery County, Pennsylvania)

A peerless example of academic Gothic design, the Goodhart is noted for its huge concrete arches, which frame the main theater space. Samuel Yellin created the amazing metalwork that can be seen throughout the venue, and its construction and design meld the historic elements of this Bryn Mawr building with beautifully contemporary touches. The perfect retro-modern hybrid.

The Teatro La Fenice (Venice, Italy)

The Teatro La Fenice motto is "rise from the ashes"; the Venice theatre suffered three catastrophic fires in 1774, 1836, and 1996, but rebuilding was completed within a year. However, the third fire was the result of arson. It destroyed the house in 1996. It reopened in 2004, after a three-year restoration. The theater's redesign was based on the look of the Luchino Visconti film *Senso*, which had been partially shot in the space; its nineteenth-century style was complemented by new rehearsal spaces, a reoutfitting of equipment with the latest technology, and an expansion of seating to a capacity of one thousand. It's noted for its brightly shaded interior and excellent acoustics.

Odeon of Herodes Atticus (the Acropolis, Athens, Greece)

Roman arches. A three-story stage structure. A semicircle seating design that accommodates nearly five thousand patrons.

This is authentic Greek theater at its finest, and the Herodeon, as local citizens call it, is rich in beautiful black and white marble. To experience a performance here is to truly revisit the past—while awash in the vitality of current dramatic work. The ideal theatrical combination.

——————CHAPTER 16 CHECKLIST——————

Get more out of what you've learned in this chapter by:

☐ Reviewing your program. Don't just look at the cast list prior to curtain; you can learn extra details about the play's personnel and text that will be very informative *after* you watch the play.

☐ Writing up a one-page review of your impressions of the play the next day. Once you've slept on a creative experience, you often see new angles, ideas, and nuances in hindsight that you'd not initially considered at the time you saw the play.

☐ Seeing another play as quickly as you can (within a few days to a week is ideal). Evaluate the second play the same way, even if it's the polar opposite in style and context from the first play you've looked at. Every play can be evaluated using the criteria above. Plus, comparing and contrasting two works in the same time frame gives you great perspective on what constitutes true dramatic quality. Enjoy!

17

Career Considerations

Once you've dipped your toes into the theatrical waters, you might find something extraordinary happening: you find you want to pursue a career as an actor, director, playwright, designer, or technician. Congratulations! With the proper preparation, enough experience, and a tireless work ethic, you can certainly make a living in the business. If you're already a theater major, you've made a serious commitment to your training, which is an admirable and necessary first step.

Indeed, many theater students choose to focus solely on their education at this point in their lives, before thinking too much about what initial professional steps need to be taken to become a working thespian. Giving the bulk of your attention to your studies is a very smart and valid idea, of course. But it can also be a wise decision, even from your freshman year of theater study, to start familiarizing yourself with key aspects of how precisely the pros score jobs as you develop your craft and skill set academically. It's actually hard to find a theater pro who *doesn't* wish he or she had started learning about core principles of the business sooner, in order to start working right out of the gate postgraduation.

So what else should you do at this stage to start pursuing your career track? What steps are necessary to take if you hope to become a well-prepared, highly employable theater pro? Let's examine some fairly simple, extremely effective avenues to travel now to become more seasoned, savvy, and informed.

MAKE THE MOST OF YOUR UNDERGRAD EDUCATION

Two words: don't coast. Theater is a highly participatory endeavor, as you're no doubt already aware. it can be tempting to hang out in the back row of your acting class because you don't really relish the idea of doing scene work and getting criticized by your teacher— after all, you know he never grades lower than a *B* no matter how much effort you (don't) put in. Well, change up that attitude, and push yourself! If the idea of performing in class makes you nervous, do it anyway (or look for a new career interest, if you think acting maybe isn't really up your flight of stairs). Work on your craft *every* chance you get.

That also means becoming well rounded. Sign up for every crew position offered on student productions—try everything technical out, even if you're the creative type. The more varied your practical experience is, the better you'll understand how the elements of a production mesh with and inform each other. This goes for academics, too; read as many plays as you can get your hands on. Also, see every student or department production you aren't involved with—the more theater you absorb, the more the art form will seep into your bones, become second nature, inspire and excite you. You need knowledge and enthusiasm to achieve success and longevity as a working thespian.

TAKE AN EARLY LOOK AT GRADUATE STUDY OPTIONS

If you think you might want to earn a master of fine arts after completing your bachelor of arts or bachelor of fine arts, start planning now. First of all, making sure your grades are top notch is a no-brainer. Do as much online research as you can about programs you might be interested in (there's a solid primer on terrific advanced training programs at the end of this chapter to get you started).

Talk with your drama department chair about his or her picks for great grad schools, and ask for advice on applying to these institutions. If your school has a grad program in theater, ask enrolled students for advice about how they prepared for extended learning. And begin to think about your financial options, in terms of how you might pay for more training. Lots of food for thought expands your options when the time comes.

LOOK INTO INTERNSHIPS AT PROFESSIONAL THEATERS

Check with your school's career center and your drama department administration office to see if theater companies or festivals you're interested in might be seeking applicants for unpaid (but experience-packed) internship opportunities. You can also research this info online and email theaters you're interested in for more information. It's key to get going quickly—you'll want to start applying in the fall for open opportunities that will happen the following summer. Know that internship spots are usually few and far between, so the situation will most likely be pretty competitive. Don't be daunted, though; put your best foot forward and go for it—an internship is a fantastic way to immerse yourself in the vibe of the working theater world.

LEARN ABOUT GETTING A THEATRICAL AGENT

If you're on an acting track especially, familiarize yourself with the basics of submitting yourself for consideration to a franchised agent.

Start by going straight to the actors' union, Actors Equity Association, at www.actorsequity.org/benefits/agencyregulations.asp. There you'll find a list of union-approved, or franchised, agents with solid reputations to choose from. When you're ready, you'll submit a headshot, résumé, and cover letter to the agencies that interest you (usually about two dozen at a time). Aspiring directors should consult the Stage Directors and Choreographers Society (www.sdcweb.org) and playwrights should check with the Dramatists Guild (www.dramatists guild.com) for up-to-date agency info and guidelines.

TRY A PROFESSIONAL AUDITION

Aspiring actors: go to an audition outside of school, and drink up the experience. A community theater show counts; so does a regional theater cattle call you read about in *Backstage*, the stage professional's employment bible. It's OK not to get cast—your goal is to do your best, see how the process plays out, and (maybe) get some feedback on your work. And if you do get cast? Congrats on your first job! Definitely take the role if you can balance the time commitment with school—you'll be off and running!

---SELECTED READINGS---

Here's some intriguing, real-world info and perspective on working in the theater, to get you thinking.

My First Job: Adrian Bridges

We first met the amazing gifted theatrical Renaissance man Adrian Bridges back in chapter 8, where he discussed his extensive sound design work. Here, Bridges shares his insight on his first acting job and his professional attitude as a whole.

Q: What was your first acting job like? What did you learn from this experience breaking into the business that has really helped you in your work ever since?*

A: My first acting job was in an adaptation of *Three Sisters*, where I played a minor character who also played the musical accompaniment to every character's breakout song in their dreams. I didn't know anyone going into the show, but I built so many close relationships over the course of the run, and our on- and offstage friendships elevated the ensemble work in the piece.

Whenever I act, I also play music in the piece, so I've always felt secure in those situations, knowing I had the most expertise in the room for a companion part of the piece. If I look foolish because I didn't go to acting school, I know the other people I'm working with are going to let things slide or tell me in a friendly way what I'm doing wrong because I can support them in other elements of the piece. As an actor, I think directors always appreciate when you're willing to go out on a limb and make a bold choice in your performance. I know every time I get kudos as an actor, it comes when I really push myself, and occasionally those things fall flat. Unless you're wiling to fail sometimes, though, you won't ever discover the most exciting moments.

Most importantly, I try to show up on time, be pleasant, and listen to both the director and other artists I'm working with. That's what really pays off. Where I usually get the most shaken working in theater is the chain of command. Music, and especially jazz and rock, which I play, tends to be a much more openly collaborative art form, so there are times where I want to talk directly to another member of the ensemble or creative team about changing something, but I have to stop myself and find a way to relay that message to the director first so they can be on top of the execution.

Beating the Butterflies, and a Whole Lot More: James Foster Jr.

James Foster Jr. is a highly respected TV, film, and theater actor currently living and working in New York City. His credits include stage roles at Arkansas Repertory Theatre, Harlem Shakespeare Festival in New York City, Woolly Mammoth and Studio Theatre in Washington, DC, and in films by illustrious directors like Spike Lee. Here, this peerlessly professional thespian shares the story of his career trajectory and offers great tips for stopping the anxiety and self-doubt so many performers suffer from.

Q: Could you speak a bit about what sparked your interest in theater?

A: The most accurate way to answer what sparked my interest in theater—thanks to hindsight—is that it was the other way around. Theater found me, and pretty early too. I was gifted with a facility of language, playing with the sound, and the "music" if you want to call it that, of words. I would visualize narratives and stagings. I would remember scenes from films and try to repeat that dialogue in real-life situations, often with hilarious consequences. And all this was happening well before I was seven years old. That said, I didn't really know what the application of these abilities would be until much later, when I would to go to see plays that were produced at the drama department of the university I attended. Then I realized that theater was what I wanted to do; and, then, the question became, how? I've been answering that question for the last forty-plus years. That's a task that never ends!

Q: What was your first acting job like? What did you learn from this experience breaking into the business that has really helped you in your work ever since?

A: My first acting job was a disaster—and a great gift. I was cast as David in James Baldwin's *The Amen Corner*. Although my degree was not in theater, I had taken acting, scene study, dance, and a lot of other classes I thought would prepare me to be an actor. I auditioned, was cast, and thought all I had to do was learn my lines and follow direction. I was a complete failure! I learned that the director's responsibility is to direct the production, not to guide you or coach your performance (you may be fortunate to have that style of director; but don't count on it). That lesson was a great gift. It taught me to bring an overload of preparation, analysis, opinions, and points of view to the first rehearsal. If I have a director whose style is very involved with the actor's process and wants to hear, and will consider using, any or all of that, fine! If, on the other hand, the director has another style, or process of working, use your preparation, and allow the director to use, discard, or edit. I should add, however, it is a collaborative effort. If there is a moment, or moments, where I feel my choice is correct, I am prepared to respectfully state my choice and justify it. I am equally prepared to do it the director's way, to the best of my ability, if my choice is rejected.

Q: What advice would you have for young actors regarding nervousness at the prospect of auditions or taking on their first jobs? How did you "beat the butterflies" early in your own career?

A: In reality, you're asking several questions. Butterflies should not be crippling or paralyzing. I need to say that right away. Think of butterflies as a gift. It's the same situation as a racehorse that gets to the gate and starts prancing and chomping on the bit. Racehorses were made to race, when it's time to do their thing. Actors act, when it's time to do their thing. Butterflies are actually your physical, mental, and emotional energy rising to the occasion. Be concerned if the time ever comes when you don't feel that little tingle or that excitement or whatever way your butterflies may manifest. I still feel it, each and every time. I look for it because it tells me my senses—physical, mental, and emotional—are ready to go to work. On auditions—it's not only nervousness because it's a new experience. It's excitement because you're finally getting a chance to do what you've dreamed of. It's sometimes anxiety because you're broke and you *really* need this paying job. And, maybe, a million other things—needing to prove to your folks that you can build a successful career, and they didn't waste their money paying for a theater degree; needing to prove to yourself the same thing; needing to get into this particular show because important agents, managers, or casting directors will probably come; I could keep going.

I have come to regard auditions like this—auditions are the real job! The number of auditions you go to will greatly exceed the number of jobs you'll be offered. And the audition begins the second you walk in the door, before you've introduced yourself, shaken hands, or started your monologue/sides. Same thing for singing or dance auditions. Make peace with it. Accept it as the business model for the profession you have chosen to pursue. Develop a good audition technique, as soon as possible. That could be auditioning for things you really are not interested in just to get comfortable with the mechanics of walking in the room, the introduction, the presentation, and the exit. Or, if necessary, take classes in audition technique. Lastly, the "temperature" of the room will change from initial audition, through each callback, because the field is narrowing, and the stakes are higher for everyone on both sides of the table. So don't expect to step in the same river twice, as the saying goes.

About first jobs—it could be argued that every job is a first job, because you're almost always working with new people, in a new location, on new material. Even if you're doing a revival of a piece with everyone intact from the initial production, it's "a first" in a sense. As I said before, auditioning is the real job. Once you're cast, it means several people in the casting process have come to the conclusion that you are the best choice for that role. Take comfort, and confidence, in that reality. Do your preparation before rehearsals begin. Be on time. Be prepared. Do your homework each night. Be kind to your coworkers. Be patient. Be supportive. Do your best job each day. Be grateful that life has given you the opportunity to live your dream.

Q: What do you love most about working in the theater?

A: I love, and am grateful for, the chance to use my gifts and abilities to bring enjoyment, pleasure, and entertainment to people. I believe the act of entertaining, or show business, is a great service and gift we provide. Storytelling, in all its many forms, has been around for as long as mankind has been in existence. Clearly it is something people have a need for and enjoy experiencing. I feel honored to be able to serve my fellow human beings.

The Gold Standard: Advanced Theater Training Programs

When it comes to learning your craft, there are good theater training programs, and then there are *great* theater training programs. Here are seven schools considered to be among the very best in the world when it comes to educating professional actors, directors, playwrights, and designers, many of whom have gone on to become award-winning, game-changing professional artists.

The American Conservatory Theatre, or ACT (www.act-sf.org) in San Francisco, California, was founded in 1967 and has a sterling reputation for both outstanding theater performance and training. Known for its fearlessly experimental productions, ACT's conservatory, led by Melissa Smith, now serves three thousand students every year and was the first actor training program in the United States not affiliated with a college or university accredited to award a master of fine arts degree. Danny Glover, Annette Bening, Denzel Washington, Benjamin Bratt, and Anika Noni Rose lead ACT's illustrious list of amazing alumni.

The Bristol Old Vic Theatre School (www.oldvic.ac.uk) in Bristol, England, is classical training at its absolute finest. The school was opened in 1946 by Laurence Olivier as the training wing for the Bristol Old Vic Company. Known the world over for producing the most dedicated and technically proficient performers, alumni include master thespians Daniel Day-Lewis, Naomie Harris, and Jeremy Irons.

Cours Florent (www.coursflorent.education) in Paris, France, teaches state-of-the-art acting technique in French, English, or German. Founder Francois Florent intended the school to be focused very individually on the talents and interests of each individual student, a practice that carries forth today. Actors who attend Cours Florent are noted for the great physical ease and movement mastery they possess after completing the program, with copious training in staging, music, and dance; many graduates have established themselves in cinema as well as theater, such as internationally celebrated film stars Isabelle Adjani, Guillaume Canet, and Daniel Auteuil. The school even has its own casting office to help students secure professional jobs during school and after graduation.

The Juilliard School (www.juilliard.edu) in New York City, located at Lincoln Center, has a peerless reputation for making the best theater students realize their full potential. Juilliard's esteemed drama division was founded in 1968 by John Houseman and Michel Saint-Denis and today offers a bachelor of fine arts, a diploma, and a master of fine arts. Juilliard is known as a tough, totally immersive program that demands excellence and turns out wonderful graduates who reflect these ideals, among them Jessica Chastain, Robin Williams, and Christopher Reeve.

The National Theatre School of Canada (ent-nts.ca/en) in Montreal boasts nine professional training programs, produces nearly two dozen student productions per year, and has prepared over two thousand professional artists for work in the entertainment industry since its inception in 1960. A great place to learn the ropes and the survival skills necessary to thrive in a business sense. Graduates include acclaimed actors Sandra Oh and Blair Brown.

The Western Australian Academy of Performing Arts at Edith Cowan University in Perth, Australia (www.waapa.ecu.edu.au) is world renowned for its comprehensive courses. The opportunity to act in over three hundred performances open to the public is another strong draw for applicants (many of these productions are done in professional venues). It is an ideal place to learn and then showcase your chops; lauded former students have included Heath Ledger, Hugh Jackman, and Frances O'Connor.

The Yale School of Drama (drama.yale.edu) in New Haven, Connecticut, is a graduate professional conservatory for acting, design (sets, costumes, lighting, projection, and sound), directing, dramaturgy and dramatic criticism, playwrighting, stage management, technical design and production, and theater management. The school works in tandem with the Yale Repertory Theatre to afford students professional work experience and is considered to be one of the most rigorous, respected training programs in the world. Distinguished alumni include Meryl Streep, Kevin Kline, Sigourney Weaver, and Lupita Nyong'o.

——————CHAPTER 17 CHECKLIST——————

Get more out of what you've learned in this chapter by:

☐ Writing yourself a career letter of intention. Sit down and write a letter to yourself, outlining all of your hopes, dreams, and goals for your career that you ideally want to achieve ten years from today. Brainstorm ways you intend to go about achieving your goals, from further study to writing your own play to networking with other thespians you know—whatever comes to mind. Then wait twenty-four hours, and read the letter over—you'll be amazed and delighted at the clarity it gives you about the path you need to take. You won't follow all of your intentions to the letter, most likely—life will guide your career, of course, to a certain extent. But you'll be so much clearer about what you want—and when you want something badly enough, you'll be just fine putting in the hard work you'll need to get it.

18

Your Production Project

Just do it! It works for when you need to amp up your sports skills, and it really works when you want to fully understand how theater, as an overall entity and process, works when all of its separate parts come together. Time to plunge in and put up your own student production!

This is an optional project, it must be said. If you're using this book as part of a general theater studies or theater theory class, it may not be course appropriate in terms of time or context to produce a show in conjunction with your classwork. In this case, consider using this chapter as a guide for putting up an extracurricular production. Now if your course is conducive to production work? Terrific! Start reading and planning.

What follows is a primer that lays out how to stage a one-act play as a class group, as a way for you and your students to put to practical use the knowledge you've gained throughout this book. There are roles for actors, a director, designers, and technicians; the basics of how to schedule and run a four-week rehearsal process, tech, and show run are fully detailed (you'll work for a total of five weeks from start to finish for this project). Following the production, we also discuss the importance of constructive feedback and outline a primer for fruitful group evaluation of the work the class has produced together.

The golden rule here: *keep everything simple.* Your direction. Your cues. Your actors' blocking. Your designs. The number of set pieces and props you use. Everything. You'll most likely be performing your play in a small space without a lot of technical bells and whistles available—that's perfectly OK. Don't try to produce the most complicated, flashy effects. Make sure your show's running time is short. In order to get the most of this experience educationally, you want to focus on the basic mechanics of putting up your show. Lack of complication will keep you from becoming distracted from this goal. Think about the core steps you'll be performing before anything else, and you'll be OK.

Ready to go? Here's the order of business.

PLANNING PERIOD (WEEK ONE)

Step One: Assemble Your Company

First of all, take a head count and decide how many students are going to be involved in your production. Let's say you've got fifteen interested parties. Now it's time to break down who will do what job. For a one-act play, figure on two to five actors as the optimum cast size. Now you need a director, a playwright or dramaturg (a student who will be in charge of choosing and interpreting the play's text), a set designer, a lighting/sound designer, a costume designer, a stage manager, and three to four crew members. That should give everyone a position to learn from.

Step Two: Choose Your Material

If your playwright has written an original one-act he or she would like to produce, great! If the better option is to choose a previously published one-act, your dramaturg and director should work together on selecting a play online or from your school library. Once they settle on a play, they should copy the pages and make hard-copy scripts for everyone. (There are copyright rules to consider if a published play is to be used. The director should take care to obtain any necessary permissions.)

Step Three: Choose Your Performance Space

A small black box theater or large rehearsal room with some technical capabilities often exists and is available at many colleges and universities. That kind of space will work just fine for a one-act performance. If your pickings are slimmer, secure the largest classroom or common area you can find, and resolve to simplify your lighting/sound and set to fit any logistical limitations. No worries—you'll quickly find that your one-act doesn't have to be too flashy or complex technically in order to teach your group a lot.

Step Four: Start the Design Process

Your designers should start putting ideas for their work down on paper, using the script and conversation with the director as guides going forth. Costume sketches, a simple lighting plot or sound ideas, and a set model are essential, even in a small space. Your director should start writing out blocking ideas as well.

Step Five: Check In with Each Other

At the end of the week, hold a meeting in which your director, designers, and stage manager meet to go over completed ideas and plan for auditions at the top of next week. The director should approve design ideas at this time, and the stage manager should begin assembling a promptbook with notes from everyone as warranted. (Tip: google "promptbook" for a sample setup as to how this binder can be created—and keep things simple! Clarity is a great teacher when you're doing a one-act. You'll just want to include a script, cast list, prop list, designer info, blocking notes within your script, and cues within your script.)

PREREHEARSAL PERIOD (WEEK TWO)

Step One: Hold a Casting Session

Your director and stage manager should ask your actors to read from the play so your director can decide who should play which role. For a class project such as this, keep the process easy and informal; gather all of your actors together around a table, and have them switch off between roles. Your director should have a pretty good idea who fits which part by the end of an hour or two. He or she can assign roles accordingly so your actors can start thinking about their characters.

Step Two: Complete Scheduling

Your stage manager and director should hold a meeting with your designers about how the rehearsal and production schedule will commence starting next week. Follow weeks three through six below for a template.

Step Three: Keep Designs Progressing

Your designers should be working on the process of building or pulling costumes and furniture already. Make sure your director is consulting with them on ideas from the start so everyone remains on the same creative page.

Step Four: Hold a Read-Through

The entire company should meet to hear your actors do a table read of the script (the end of the week is ideal for this, as your performers will have had a few days to think about their concepts for their roles).

During this week, your director should also make individual appointments with each actor to talk about their characters—answering questions the actor has, talking about the character's backstory if that's something the actor wants to do—basically, helping the actor start to form the direction he or she wants to take).

PHYSICAL REHEARSAL PERIOD (WEEKS THREE AND FOUR)

Step One: Blocking

Plan three days for the director's process of blocking out your actors' movements onstage. Your actors and your stage manager should take notes in your scripts so you remember these movements. Your actors also want to start memorizing their lines, if they haven't started already. They should shoot to be off-book by the start of week four, by the way.

Step Two: Scene Work

The remaining two days of this week should consist of beginning to practice the blocking, work through any questions or issues regarding the text with your playwright or dramaturg, and direct the actors' performances. Your designers and technical crew should watch as much of these rehearsals as they have time for, as this will help inform their work as they continue to build, pull, and refine their designs.

Step Three: Walk-Throughs and Run-Throughs

By the start of week four, your cast should be off-book. For the first three days of week four, finish all scene work and begin performing your one-act in sequence. Actors should walk through the play, and your director should stop them as often as needed to give direction and make adjustments.

By day four and five of week four, the cast should start running through the one-act start to finish without stopping. This will be a clumsy, messy process at first—that's to be expected. The directors should address all mistakes in notes and give them at the end of rehearsal.

TECH AND DRESS REHEARSAL PERIOD (WEEK FIVE)

Step One: Designer Load-In

Day one: Your designers should have completed their work by now. Your set designer should assemble the set with your stage manager and any crew he or she has; your costume designer should have your cast members try on all wardrobe and accessories; and your lighting and sound designer should work with your stage manager to start writing cues.

Step Two: Final Run-Through

Day two: Your director will run through the show one final time before tech rehearsals.

Step Three: Dry Tech

Day three: Run through the show's technical cues without the actors present and with your technicians learning and executing cues.

Step Four: Wet Tech

Day four: Run through the show with full tech and actors inserted.

Step Five: Dress Rehearsal

On day five, pull all the elements together: the actors are in costume, and the show is fully teched. This is the show you're going to present!

PERFORMANCE PERIOD (WEEK SIX)

Schedule three to five performances. Invite your fellow theater class-mates, teachers, and friends. At the end of every performance, ask everyone to stay, and offer constructive feedback. This can be an ex-tremely worthwhile enterprise in terms of immediate reaction to and opinion of what you've done. If you agree with an audience member's suggestion and your company wants to implement it, feel free to do so. If you choose to ignore the feedback, that's fine, too. Either way, you gain information and perspective.

At the end of your last performance, hold a cast meeting, and do a group evaluation of the production as a whole. Open up the floor, and ask your company members to discuss what they loved about doing the production, what they didn't love so much, what they learned, and what they'll know to do better next time.

Now . . . strike as a group! And start thinking about the *next* show you want to do.

———————CHAPTER 18 CHECKLIST———————

Remember these quick tips as you move through the production process—they'll enhance your learning experience.

1. Again—simplify!

If something starts feeling unwieldy or complicated, cut it out of the show. It's most likely a time and attention waster.

2. Shoot for clarity.

Always make sure lines are loud and clear, your backdrop isn't too busy, and your blocking is logical in terms of how your characters would realistically move. The clearer your production is, the more impact it will have on your audience.

3. When in doubt, drill it.

Got an extra five minutes? Run through that problem scene again. And again. Practice gets the bugs out—no shortcuts.

4. Please yourselves first.

Don't worry about what people will think of what you're doing while you're in the production process. It's a limiting attitude, and you won't end up doing your best work.

5. Learn from every aspect of the experience.

The good, the bad, and everything in the middle. Be open, give the show your best shot, and you can't go wrong.

19

Using Your Theater Education (in Ways You Never Thought Of)

On a personal note, as the author of this book: I've been lucky to have had many tremendous, exciting, educational, creative, and fulfilling experiences in the theater myself. During my long career as a theater performer, playwright, teacher, director, and writer, I've also been privileged to speak in depth with scores of theater students and theater educators. A very interesting, and common, point of discussion these folks have engaged in with me has to do with what one can really do with a theater education, outside of a traditional creative or technical career track. Is studying theater worthwhile if you don't necessarily see a future for yourself onstage or backstage?

Absolutely, and this is such a great topic to explore. In my opinion, studying theater can be a true asset for almost everyone choosing their life's work. A dramatic skill can deftly prepare a student for a huge range of different jobs, not to mention help them handle many different workplace challenges and situations. Studying theater can build or strengthen a number of crucial qualities we all need professionally, including the following.

Emotional Intelligence

As a student actor, director, or playwright, learning to analyze the emotions and decisions of a character you're creating is of course essential. Without your even realizing it, the more character study you do, the more this kind of analysis builds empathy, perception, and simpatico thinking toward other people.

Confidence

Acting especially helps you shed personal inhibitions, shyness, and feelings of social intimidation. Think about it: it's a pretty brave action to share deep emotions with an audience of friends *and* strangers. You deserve to feel proud of this accomplishment, and let it fuel you with self-assurance.

Creative Problem Solving

Any type of theater study helps you think faster, and more effectively, on your feet, due to the fact that you're learning to meld both creative and technical mental motion at the same time. Theater is also an art form that's guaranteed *not* to run smoothly a good percentage of the time—that's why directors and stage managers tend to be experts at putting out fires. Thinking out new ways to deal effectively with pop-up issues is par for the course and good training for any other work you can think of.

Ease with Public Speaking

Theater study can inspire even an extrovert to become more outgoing quickly when he or she sees just how much fun expressing yourself onstage can be. And since speaking to groups is important in so many types of professional careers today—from speaking at a conference to acing a presentation—feeling comfortable is a truly valuable skill to have in your pocket.

OUT-OF-THE-BOX THEATER-RELATED CAREERS

Which brings us to specific arts-related work prospects theater study can be especially beneficial for, aside from the commonly considered fields of acting, directing, playwrighting, or teching. Theater majors know that there are a number of fascinating avenues one can pursue in terms of careers related to their education, including the following.

Arts Administration

You can opt to be an artistic director, a university administrator, a business administrator, a union representative—there are so many positions that require the creative experience of theater training, plus practical business acumen.

Teaching

Many theater teachers are also working theater professionals or have previously worked professionally as actors, designers, playwrights, or technicians. There's no better way to pass on hard-won personal experience and knowledge.

Theater Journalism

Working as a critic, author, or magazine/newspaper journalist is a terrific way to use the extensive factual knowledge gained in theater study to recognize new talent and cover important issues in today's entertainment industry.

Public Relations

Theater training is a great way to learn good communication skills, a must for PR professionals in virtually any business or specific company role.

Theatrical Company/Product Sales

Hands-on know-how is key for any job at a theatrical supply or service company. The good news: there are lots of companies out there and plentiful openings most of the time.

Theater Transportation

If you've studied set design and done student set construction or set run, why not put your skill set to work as a supervisor for a theater production transport company? Or start your own theater trucking firm specializing in load-ins and strikes—it can be a very profitable and satisfying lifestyle if you love to travel.

OTHER CAREER POSSIBILITIES OUTSIDE OF THEATER-RELATED WORK

Here are some excellent prospects in a variety or professional disciplines; theater training can help you prosper in any of them.

Sales

Interested in a position requiring selling techniques and dealing with the public? Acting experience can obviously help you here.

Law

Delivering an impassioned case before a jury can be a whole lot easier if you've got some performance study under your belt.

Medicine

Feeling comfortable interacting with patients on a one-to-one level can be made a lot easier if you've taken an acting class or two. Doctors in training also often role-play patient interactions with professional actors today, so there's lots of good evidence that performance experience can be useful to them.

Teaching Any Subject Besides Theater

Any type of teaching, on any grade or collegiate level, requires you to engage your students. Theater training can help you gain the skills to do this seamlessly.

Business

Making a good impression in meetings, during the aforementioned important presentation, while giving a professional keynote speech—theater training can, as we previously covered, boost your confidence and ensure your success.

And these are just a few possibilities of careers that you can pursue. Sit down and brainstorm a list of jobs you could see yourself really enjoying—then jot down ways your theater training could help you in any of these career possibilities. No doubt you'll see the advantages you have going after virtually *any* goal.

THEATER TRAINING HELPS FUEL ANY AMBITION

Lastly, remember this important truth: studying drama is a wonderful way to become a more a well-rounded person. It can also help you realize any dream you have to the fullest. Why? Studying theater makes you bold. You've felt the thrill of surpassing your own expectations for yourself, of showing emotional honesty, of sharing your imagination, of sticking your neck out creatively. These things take courage—and courage is what we all need to achieve our deepest aspirations.

Use the theatrical tools you've learned in class, and in this book, as practically as you want and need to as you go forward in your education and, eventually, your chosen career. May you stay brave and gain all the future happiness and success you seek. Break a leg!

Appendixes

APPENDIX A

Ten Plays Every Theater Student Should Read and/or See

Each of these straight dramatic plays defines the pinnacle of excellence.

Angels in America by Tony Kushner
A sweeping commentary on AIDS, discrimination, self-acceptance, death, and doing the right thing.

Arcadia by Tom Stoppard
An emotional time-traveling epic, from the 1800s to modern day.

Betrayal by Harold Pinter
A deftly written, searing dissection of a relationship.

Cat on a Hot Tin Roof by Tennessee Williams
A passionate parable, filled with conflict, rejection, secrets, and high dramatic tension.

The Crucible by Arthur Miller
The Salem witch trials serve as a powerful metaphor for the importance of preserving civil liberties in this highly dramatic and emotional masterpiece.

Curse of the Starving Class by Sam Shepard
A tragic American family morality lesson.

The Life and Adventures of Nicholas Nickleby by David Edgar and
    Stephen Oliver
Based on Charles Dickens's book, the play is long (eight and a half hours of stage running time!), but a completely absorbing examination of capitalism for the greater good.

Romeo and Juliet by William Shakespeare
The classic tale of star-crossed love.

Three Tall Women by Edward Albee
An unflinchingly honest look at the relationships between three women at different points in their lives and how they relate to themselves and each other. Bold and challenging.

Uncommon Women and Others by Wendy Wasserstein
A fascinating depiction of feminist issues as wrestled with by college classmates at a reunion.

APPENDIX B

Ten Musicals Every Theater Student Should Read and/or See

These melodic masterpieces are full of substance and beauty.

Carousel by Oscar Hammerstein II and Richard Rodgers
A decades-old romance doomed by economic strife that remains socially significant today.

Chicago by Bob Fosse, Fred Ebb, and John Kander
A tale of celebrity, violence, unethical behavior, and where all of it can get you—great social commentary.

Company by Stephen Sondheim
A man's midlife crisis hits all the right realistic notes and is a great example of confessional songwriting at its best.

Dear Evan Hansen by Benj Pasek, Justin Paul, and Steven Levenson
A touching story of the need for true connection in the millennial world.

Evita by Tim Rice and Andrew Lloyd Webber
The thrilling life and times of Argentinian first lady and icon Eva Peron—this is the musical at its most commanding.

Guys and Dolls by Frank Loesser, Jo Swerling, and Abe Burrows
The frothy love story between a gambler and a missionary that stands the test of time as few theater pieces can.

Hair by Gerome Ragni and Galt MacDermot
A lively time capsule of '60s hippie lifestyle and philosophy.

Hamilton: An American Musical by Lin-Manuel Miranda
You've read about it previously in this book, and it must be lauded again: perhaps the greatest modern example of truly engaging musical theater material.

Les Misérables by Alain Boublil and Claude-Michel Schönberg
The epic trajectory of Jean Valjean, a man who is the epitome of good in a dark, evil world.

Rent by Jonathan Larson
A pitch-perfect portrait of urban blight and the will to survive in 1990s New York City.

APPENDIX C

Publications That Serious Theater Students Should Check Out Regularly

Want to know more about the business of theater? These highly respected sources are packed with up-to-the-minute info on key movers and shakers, job openings, industry news, and productions in the pipeline.

Backstage
www.backstage.com

Stage Directions **Magazine**
www.stage-directions.com

Broadway.com
www.broadway.com

Theater Mania
www.theatermania.com

Broadway World
www.broadwayworld.com

Variety
www.variety.com

APPENDIX D

Resources for Students Who Want to Make Great Educational Theater

Here are some great organizations whose mission is to encourage young playmakers to express themselves. Check out their websites; you'll find advice and assistance on everything from choosing the right high school play to produce to scholarship opportunities, mentorship info, and career planning.

American Theatre Wing (home of the Tony Awards)
www.americantheatrewing.org

Educational Theatre Association
www.schooltheatre.org

Music Theatre International
www.mtishows.com

Theatre Development Fund
www.tdf.org

APPENDIX E

Five Great Theaters to Visit in Person

These houses present challenging, thought-provoking material, and boast some great history, too. Hit the road—you'll learn a lot!

American Repertory Theater
Cambridge, Massachusetts
www.americanrepertorytheater.org
Known for its avant-garde productions, as well as its educational affiliation with Harvard University, ART's esteemed list of collaborators has included directors Robert Wilson and Diane Paulus, playwright David Mamet, and composer Philip Glass.

The Belasco Theatre
New York, New York
www.shubert.nyc/theatres/belasco
This mysterious, old school, glamorously ancient Broadway house has not only been around for decades—it's rumored to be haunted by

a ghost who sits in the audience. Great actors have tread the boards here, including Denzel Washington and Ralph Fiennes in Shakespeare's *Julius Caesar* and *Hamlet* respectively (ghost or no ghost).

Ford's Theatre
Washington, DC
www.fords.org
The site of President Abraham Lincoln's assassination not only serves as a national landmark and educational center but also produces wonderful shows on political and historical subjects throughout the year.

The Geffen Playhouse
Los Angeles, California
www.geffenplayhouse.org
Founded by the late theater, film, and TV producer and professor Gilbert Cates, the Geffen encourages respected film performers, from Annette Bening to Brooke Shields to the late Carrie Fisher, to stretch creatively onstage in both original and well-known pieces of work. Always an illuminating night at the theater.

The John F. Kennedy Center for the Performing Arts
Washington, DC
www.kennedycenter.org
The jewel of America's creative crown. The Kennedy Center produces original productions, offers educational opportunities, hosts pre-Broadway tryouts—virtually every kind of theater that could interest you is done here and done at its best.

Index

Books from Allworth Press

Acting
by Terry Schreiber with Mary Beth Barber (6 × 9, 256 pages, paperback, $19.95)

Acting the Song (Second Edition)
by Tracey Moore with Allison Bergman (6 × 9, 336 pages, paperback, $24.99)

Actor Training the Laban Way
by Barbara Adrian (7⅜ × 9¼, 208 pages, paperback, $24.95)

The Actor Uncovered
by Michael Howard (6 × 9, 240 pages, paperback, $19.99)

An Actor's Guide: Making It in New York City (Second Edition)
by Glenn Alterman (6 × 9, 344 pages, paperback, $24.95)

An Actor's Guide: Your First Year in Hollywood (Fourth Edition)
by Michael St. Nicholas and Lisa Mulcahy (6 × 9, 316 pages, paperback, $19.99)

Broadway General Manager
by Peter Bogyo (6 × 9, 240 pages, hardcover, $29.99)

Business and Legal Forms for Theater, Second Edition
by Charles Grippo (8½ x 11, 192 pages, paperback, $24.95)

The Business of Broadway
by Mitch Weiss and Perri Gaffney (6 x 9, 292 pages, hardcover, $24.99)

Clues to Acting Shakespeare (Third Edition)
by Wesley Van Tassel (6 × 9, pages, 344 paperback, $18.99)

Creating Your Own Monologue (Second Edition)
by Glenn Alterman (6 × 9, 256 pages, paperback, $19.99)

The Health and Safety Guide for Film, TV, and Theater (Second Edition)
by Monona Rossol (6 × 9, 288 pages, paperback, $27.50)

Leadership in the Performing Arts
by Tobie S. Stein (5½ × 8¼, 252 pages, paperback, $19.99)

A Life in Acting
by Lisa Mulcahy (6 × 9, 192 pages, paperback, $16.95)

The Lucid Body
by Fay Simpson (6 × 9, 224 pages, paperback, $19.95)

Making It on Broadway
by David Wienir and Jodie Langel (6 x 9, 288 pages, paperback, $19.95)

Movement for Actors (Second Edition)
Edited by Nicole Potter, Mary Fleischer, and Barbara Adrian (6 × 9, 376 pages, paperback, $22.99)

The Perfect Stage Crew (Second Edition)
by John Kaluta (6 × 9, 272 pages, paperback, $19.99)

Starting Your Career as an Actor
by Jason Pugatch (6 × 9, 320 pages, paperback, $19.95)

Your Child's Career in Music and Entertainment
by Steven C. Beer with Kathryne Badura (5½ × 8¼, 184 pages, paperback, $14.99)

To see our complete catalog or to order online, please visit www.allworth.com.